YORUBA DRAMA IN ENGLISH
Interpretation and Production

J.B. Alston

Studies in African Literature
Volume 1

The Edwin Mellen Press
Lewiston/Lampeter/Queenston

Library of Congress Cataloging-in-Publication Data

Alston, J.B.
  Yoruba drama in English : interpretation and production / J.B. Alston.
    p. cm. -- (Studies in African literature ; v. 1)
  Bibliography: p.
  Includes index.
  ISBN 0-88946-726-9
  1. Nigerian drama (English)--Yoruba authors--History and
criticism. 2. Nigerian drama (English)--20th century--History and
criticism. 3. Theater--Nigeria--History--20th century. 4. Yoruba
(African people)--Intellectual life. 5. Yoruba (African people) in
literature. I. Title. II. Series : Studies in African literature
(Lewiston, N.Y.) ; v. 1.
  PR9387.3.A47 1989
  822--dc19   88-34185

┌───┐
│ This is volume 1 in the continuing series   │
│ Studies in African Literature   │
│ Volume 1 ISBN 0-88946-726-9   │
│ SAfL Series ISBN 0-88946-725-0   │
└───┘

A CIP catalog record for this book
is available from the British Library.

The Edwin Mellen Press   The Edwin Mellen Press
Box 450   Box 67
Lewiston, NY   Queenston, Ontario
USA   14092   CANADA   L0S 1L0

The Edwin Mellen Press, Ltd.
Lampeter, Dyfed, Wales,
UNITED KINGDOM SA48 7DY

Printed in the United States of America

TABLE OF CONTENTS

YORUBA DRAMA IN ENGLISH
Interpretation and Production

INTRODUCTION

THE NECCESSITY FOR CLARIFICATION

The growing frequency with which African drama is being produced in the United States demands that the producers bring a bit more than the most superficial generalized understanding to their productions. In the past many producers found it sufficient simply to emphasize the play's exoticism and spectacle with no attempt at analyzing the play's thematic or ideological content. It is indeed true that due to past shortages of reference materials many analytical attempts at penetrating the mysteries of African drama would have ended in frustration or misconceptions. It would, of course, make production research easier if criticism preceded drama. However, since the reverse is true, we must often wait for what seems like an interminable period of time for worthwhile analysis and criticism.

Fortunately for western producers we are beginning to see the rapid growth of criticism concerning one of the most popular forms of African drama. The popularity of Nigeria's Yoruba Drama in English has steadily grown since the late 1950s. Yet, it is only in the past decade or so that we have seen enough analysis and criticism to afford fruitful research.

Honest interpretation of dramatic thought should be as important to the producer as it is to the classroom professor. However, due to the time constraints of most

production cycles, there is little opportunity for
in-depth research. A handy reference which work seeks to
clarify the drama's key aspects should be quite welcome.
The study set forth here is intended to serve as such a
work. It will not only deal with the obvious mysteries
that may occur in the dramas but also how these elements
affect plot, thematic content, and technical
considerations. The work may also be used as an
introduction by those who are not familiar with Yoruba
drama.

To illustrate the need for such a work, let us
consider the difficulties encountered during the
university production of two African dramas in English.
The dramas, BOESMAN AND LENA by Athol Fugard (South
African) and DEATH AND THE KING'S HORSEMAN by Wole
Soyinka (Yoruba), were produced at North Carolina Central
University in 1981 and 1983 respectively.

BOESMAN AND LENA concerns the effect of Apartheid on
the existence of a husband and wife. Without becoming too
involved in plot, note these concerns that are peculiar
to this particular play. It was impossible to rehearse
BOESMAN AND LENA comfortably without answering the
following questions. Under the system of Apartheid
Boesman and Lena are classified as "coloured." Will there
be any attempt by the actors at mastering the unique
accent of South African "coloureds?" What are the
subtleties that exist in the relationship of South
African "coloureds" and South African blacks? The
question must be answered before the relationship among
Boesman, Lena, and the character known as Old African can
be properly interpreted. While he is on stage Old African
speaks only Xhosa. Fortunately the translation is
provided. However, when Xhosa is spoken there is a unique
clicking sound. Without offering a course in phonics or
an analysis of the Xhosa physical make-up, the producer
should be made aware that a language coach will certainly

be needed. During the course of the play Boesman builds a makeshift shelter called a pondok. What does it look like and how difficult is it to construct? These are only a few of the concerns that demand special attention.

Fortunately for this particular production the director was able to cast a South African in the role of Lena. The actress was able to clarify many of the subtle mysteries that plagued the production. She was, however, unable to assist with Old African's Xhosa. The search for a language coach continued until almost three weeks into rehearsal.

The experience with BOESMAN AND LENA in 1981 prompted the 1983 production staff to hire a Yoruba consultant for the production of DEATH AND THE KING'S HORSEMAN. They were able to obtain the services of Mr Shola Olaoye, a well-known musician in Yoruba literary and artistic circles. Though Soyinka attempted to minimize problems of production and interpretation, there remained a great need for the consultant. One example of Mr Olaoye's help was his explanation of the Praise-Singer's character. There is no exact equivalent in western tradition, and the actor cast in the role was having difficulty understanding the concept. In addition, the actor portraying the king was unable to interpret many of the parables and sayings spoken by his character. In order to clarify many of these questions it was necessary for Mr. Olaoye to explain the myth upon which the play's death ritual is based. Few members of the production staff realized how important myth and religion is in the life of the Yoruba. Along with his explanation of the myth and its importance, Mr. Olaoye's consultation ranged from defining single terms to resolving many problems similar to the ones found in BOESMAN AND LENA.

Though this study is limited to Yoruba drama in English, the references to BOESMAN AND LENA suggest the need for such studies in all African drama produced in the west.

SELECTION CRITERIA

This study will deal with all aspects of the plays chosen for the study and not just those which are uniquely Yoruba. The results are not to be used as a rigid production schematic from which there can be no deviation. The various aspects of a drama such as technique, language, theme, and staging, are inter-related and should be analyzed as a whole as well as separately. These concerns will not require that the production staff possess the skills of a social anthropologist. It is quite easy to fall into the "Yoruba Trap" which makes it easy to attribute all production difficulties to the fact that the play is Yoruba. In the heat of production that amount of analysis which facilitates a smooth creative production cycle is sufficient. Many producers will be surprised to find that though the content or sentiment of the plays is Yoruba, the facade or outward form is western. The majority of the Yoruba dramas in English retain the Aristotelian form so familiar in the West, and on the whole the plays will prove to be neither less functional nor less entertaining than their western counterparts.

The promotional potential of a play's production is at least equal to any other method of promotion. It is for this reason that this study will reflect a production bias. If the production of Yoruba drama in English can be made less difficult, it is then likely that the frequency of production will increase. An increase in production will, in turn, lead to increased exposure and more intense analysis of ideological and philosophical concerns.

In keeping with the practical intent of the study the criteria used for play selection had to be as prudent as possible. I have, of course, chosen only plays that are written in English and, despite the preceding statement concerning form, many of the plays would severely strain the physical limits of an average western production. Therefore, the plays chosen had to be compatible with practical western production techniques. Of equal concern were the plays written for specific occasions or locales. Many of them are rather limited in scope and so overflow with indigenous practices and concerns that they hold little or no production interest for non-Yoruba audiences. [1]

Also eliminated were those plays which were intended primarily for radio or television and adaptations of western works which would offer only slight production problems. [2] Included in the study are fifteen plays by five playwrights.

NOTES

INTRODUCTION

1

An example of such a play is Soyinka's A DANCE OF THE FORESTS. Written for the 1960 Nigerian independence celebration, the play is deeply immersed in Yoruba religious mythology. Being created for such a specific purpose causes the play to be excessively specialized in parts. At times even the stage directions are more literary than they are dramatically practical. An example is a description of Adenebi's actions at the end of Part One. "There is a crash, the noise stops suddenly, and the lights go out. Adenebi's scream being heard above it and after, stopping suddenly as he hears his own terror in the silence."

2

Examples of omitted adaptations include Rotimi's adaptation of OEDIPUS REX (THE GODS ARE NOT TO BLAME) and Soyinka's adaptations of THE THREEPENNY OPERA (OPERA WONYOSI) and THE BACCHAE (THE BACCHAE OF EURIPIDES: A COMMUNION RITE). All three plays are certainly worthy of production. However, with the possible exception of THE BACCHAE OF EURIPIDES, they would not present the same type nor as great a number of production difficulties as other plays. OPERA WONYOSI is very close to THREEPENNY OPERA in plot and character. THE BACCHAE OF EURIPIDES offers a fresh interpretation with regard to character.

I

THE RESEARCH

A CHRONOLOGICAL VIEW OF AVAILABLE RESEARCH

Early studies done on the Yoruba were conducted by Christian missionaries during the initial phases of colonial occupation. Many of these observations were understandably colored by the religious zeal of the observer. Very few were conducted with any scientific outlook or concern. Many were little more than explanatory footnotes to progress reports being sent to the mother church.

In the early 1900s explorers like Leo Frobenius started to publish accounts of their expeditions. Few of these men could even be considered qualified anthropologists, and many of them accepted appearance for reality with no attempt at verification. An excellent example of this tendency is Frobenius' comparison of Ile-Ife, the Yorubas' ancestral home, to the "Lost Atlantis" of Plato. [1]

In the years prior to World War II there was little diplomatic interest in Africa. The continent was viewed largely as an extension of Europe which displayed only economic interest. The war, however, forced the colonial powers, including the United States, to focus more attention on Africa. Despite the fact that this increased interest was for military reasons, the resulting studies in African languages and attempts at understanding African cultures generated the broader attention that the continent deserved.

For two decades before the war and for some time afterwards, the scholars who did research on the Yoruba were anthropologists. Men such as Geoffry Parrinder, Daryll Forde, William Bascom, and A.K. Ajisafe were the leaders in their field. Many of their works are considered to be quite valuable. Whatever mention there may have been of Yoruba drama, however, was made only in its relationship to particular rites, rituals, and social behavior. [2]

It was during the postwar period between 1956 and 1969 that colonial Africa underwent its greatest changes. During this period thirty-seven African states achieved independence. Suddenly the rest of the world found the prospect of political, economic, and social ties with these new nations to be irresistible. It is here that we also see the growth of the African humanist. From throughout Europe and America men like Gerald Moore, Ulli Beier, J. John, Robert Armstrong, and John Povey offered their criticism of Yoruba art and literature. Because these men were trained in literature and not in drama, most of their criticism is literary and not dramatic. [3]

In the 1960s many questions were raised concerning the value of western criticism when applied to Africa. This was a period marked by the realization that a vast number of Americans and Europeans drew their heritage from Africa. There was a push for African studies geared to the exploration of African history, society, art, literature, folklore, and music. Couple these activities with a general concern for human and civil rights and it becomes clear why the 1960s accelerated change and development. The greatest concern among Africans and those deeply involved with the study of Africa was the western critics' lack of natural or intuitive knowledge of African culture. The problems were described by J.O. Okpaku in 1978.

In some cases, in fact, this limited acquaintance with Africa produced a Western brand of that misguided Western intellectual sixth sense--the distorted notion that the West is the world and the world is the West and that whatever is worth comprehending in the non-Western world must be comprehensible within the framework of Western cultural assumptions. These assumptions were often referred to as "universal principles." The critics plagued by this malady rejected outright the relevance of culture in criticism. Bestowing on each other such tribal titles as "dean of African literature" or "leading expert on African literature," and choosing amongst their ancestors, such luminaries as Aristotle, Shakespeare, Yeats, Conrad, Sartre, and others for their patron saints, they promptly proceeded to subjugate African arts to the intrinsically ethnocentric canons of western criticism, to the battle cry of "universal aesthetics." Subsequently African arts were thinned down to fit into the pigeon holes of western criticism. Put more vividly, African art became colonized by western aesthetics. [4]

Though Okpaku's statement is true, some of what he describes was unavoidable. Even if every western critic had accepted the relevance of culture to criticism, the problem would have remained virtually the same. Even those western critics who chose to live and work in Africa could not adequately relay all of the intricacies of African culture. Short of completely refraining from the criticism of African art, it was impossible to totally eliminate the problem. There were well-known western critics who agreed with Okpaku and stated as much. Such an admission was made in 1966 in the opening statement of an article by Martin Esslin.

> I must at the very outset, disclaim any special knowledge of the social and cultural background from which these plays spring. That, indeed, I presume, must have been the reason I was to review them in these pages--to provide, for once, the corrective of a change of perspective, as it were; of focus, of viewpoint to submit them, like organisms in a laboratory, to a survival test "in vacuo" by seeing how they appear to someone who in the course of his professional work has to read an endless succession of plays from totally different backgrounds, and who will therefore, almost automatically, apply to them the same general yardstick; who will judge them not as African but as plays pure and simple.
> Having said this, I am bound to add that I think such a test hardly possible. It may be so with poetry, which deals with the basic human emotions on a purely individual plane: affection, loneliness, joy, sorrow and the skills with which they are expressed might be truly universal. But drama deals with the basic human emotions and predicaments in a social context, both in the interaction of several characters on the stage, and in the even more important interaction between stage and audience. The basic human emotions are still involved, but they are expressed through social conventions which may be totally different from one society to another.[5]

For those concerned with African studies, an answer to the problem of cultural relevance began to emerge in the mid-sixties. During this period the world of criticism experienced rapid growth in the number of African critics. These scholars held important advantages over their western predecessors. Not only were they trained in their respective disciplines, but they also possessed that all important intuitive knowledge of the cultures which were producing an ever increasing number of creative works. This proliferation of African scholarship has, in the past decade, produced a dependable body of resource materials for those concerned with African studies. Yet, for the western researcher interested in African drama it is only recently that Africans have begun to study drama as other than a minor form of literature. Much of the initial criticism has come from the same men who are creating the dramatic works. This is especially true of Yoruba drama in English. The critical essays and other works of playwrights such as Soyinka, Omotoso, and Rotimi comprise a good deal of the available research. Recently, the works of African scholars with varying degrees of training in the discipline have begun to emerge. Foremost among them are Oyin Ogunba, A.O. Ashaolu, Joel Adedeji, Femi Osofisan, Dapo Adelugba, and Oyekan Owomoyela. The direct criticism of these Nigerians along with peripheral studies by other African scholars such as East African critic Peter Nazareth and South African critic B.L. Leshosi, and selected criticism by western writers, has produced an adequate body of material for research in Yoruba drama in English. [6]

THE STATE OF YORUBA THEATRE

Nearly two decades ago, in 1966, leading Yoruba critic Oyin Ogunba made the following statement concerning the state of Nigerian theatre.

> There is not a single respectable public
> playhouse in Nigeria. What we have are
> make-shift schoolrooms, dining-halls and club
> houses like the Mbari used as theatres. There
> was a cry for national theatre, even in the
> 1880s, and this cry has continued off-and-on
> since that time, but with no positive result.
> Perhaps the failure of our dramatists to
> produce masterpieces to date is attributable
> to the fact that the theatre is not popular;
> the artist does not feel a tumultuous
> excitement at his work, as a man the community
> wants--the cinema is infinitely more popular.
> The Nigerian theatre has not yet come to stay:
> it still looks forward to the time when
> Nigerian peoples, other than the Yoruba, will
> develop dramas in their own languages: when the
> playwrights in English will not just feel like
> a shipwrecked man on a lonely island, talking
> ineffectually to the winds. [7]

More than a decade later, in 1978, Yoruba critic
J.O. Okpaku expressed similar concerns.

> It should be noted that the establishment of
> drama department in university is a recent
> phenomenon, and exists mostly in U.S.
> universities. In British and French
> universities, which until recently accounted
> directly and indirectly for most of the
> education of Africans, it is still a rarity.
> The study of drama as a profession was regarded
> in parts of Africa, until recently, as being "a
> joke." [8]

Today, some seven years later, it is, of course, not possible to report that the concerns quoted above have all been addressed and that the Yoruba theatre flourishes on an equal footing with the rest of the world. It can be reported, however, that there has been steady progress and that the Yoruba theatre in English has a great deal to do with that progress.

The Yoruba playwrights in English feel much less like "a shipwrecked man on a lonely island, talking ineffectually to the winds." They are no longer plagued by the pointless controversy concerning their choice of language. Their acceptance in the West is broadening while their efforts at home are becoming better understood and appreciated. Later chapters will reveal the extent to which their art has progressed. Its support and continued development is virtually assured by the overall theatrical activity in Nigeria. This energetic refinement is creating a unique theatric tradition in which Yoruba drama in English will occupy a prominent position.

An example of this continuing refinement has to do with the physical theatre in Nigeria. There is, as will be pointed out in later chapters, some concern for proper staging facilities. Much of the drama done in Yorubaland is not well suited to the limitations found in western theatre architecture. There is a search for a facility which lends itself to a fluid free-flowing form which lacks the assumed barriers between actors and audience that are inherent in proscenium houses. The few permanent theatre houses which do exist in Nigeria were, like many American theatres, designed with what Martin Banham refers to as "a mixture of nostalgia and nonsense." Proof that this problem is well on the way to being solved can be seen in the work of Demas Nwoko, a Nigerian theatrical designer and architect who has designed small centers which are more conducive to the production of Yoruba drama. [9]

Further signs of positive progress exist in the continuing leadership of the universities which have for years been in the forefront of dramatic development. Most of the leading playwrights and critics are closely connected with the universities which still provide sources of finance and raw talent. The increase in the number of drama groups, such as Bode Sowande's Odu Themes groups in Ibadan is also encouraging.

In the past necessity forced many playwrights to direct and take the lead in the productions of their plays. In recent years there has been an increase in theatre directors, actors, and designers. These younger practitioners display a good deal of talent. They include director-composers Sonny Oti and Tunji Vidal and actors Gbemi Sodipe and Segun Bankole.

The obvious potential of the Yoruba theatre in English is continuously being fulfilled. Once we see the establishment of a mutually supportive relationship between the indigenous theatre and the theatre in English, there will be an acceleration of the maturation of both, which will result in a strong theatrical institution.

NOTES

CHAPTER ONE

1
Leo Frobenius, THE VOICE OF AFRICA (LONDON: Hutchinson, 1913) Vol.I p. 344f.

2
The principal modern writers with background in the social sciences and extensive study of the Yoruba are Daryll Forde, William Bascom, and Peter Lloyd. The best general introduction to the Yoruba as a group and to their culture is part four of an ethnographic survey of Africa. Part four is entitled THE YORUBA-SPEAKING PEOPLES OF SOUTH-WESTERN NIGERIA. The survey is edited by Forde and part four on the Yoruba was written by him. He addresses a wide range of subjects including ethic groupings, language, and political structure.
        William Bascom has published smaller, more detailed studies on subjects ranging from Yoruba food and cooking to the operation of lending institutions. The majority of his works were published in the early fifties by the International African Institute.
        Those interested in a sociologists' point of view should consult Peter Lloyd's THE YORUBA OF NIGERIA. The work is similar to Forde's and was published in 1965 in James Gibbs' PEOPLES OF AFRICA.
        Geoffrey Parrinder's WEST AFRICAN RELIGION and A.K. Ajisafe's THE LAWS AND CUSTOMS OF THE YORUBA PEOPLE are also worthwhile.

3
Many of these men were labeled in Joseph Okpaku's 1978 dissertation as being "extramural intellectuals," "culture adventurists," and "charlatans." It should be pointed out, however, that though many of their works might be suspect many of them are quite informative and useful when seen in their proper perspective as works of cultural observation by outside observers. This is especially true of Ulli Beier and Gerald Moore. As questionable as their motives might be, these men provided a transitional bridge between the non-literary studies of the early 1900s and the culturally competent African critics of the 1960s.

4
J.O. Okpaku, "From Swamp Dwellers to Madmen and Specialists," Diss., Standford Univ., 1978, p. 3.

16

5
Martin Esslin, "Two African Playwrights," BLACK ORPHEUS, no. 19, 1966, p. 33.

6
Relevant criticisms by these writers can be found in the bibliography.

7
Oyin Ogunba, "Theatre in Nigeria," PRESENCE AFRICAINE, no. 58, 1966, p. 88.

8
Okpaku, p. 3

9
Martin Banham, AFRICAN THEATRE TODAY (London: Pitman Publishing, 1976), p. 5.

II

BRIDGING THE ABYSS

WOLE SOYINKA

The metaphor used in this chapter's subtitle is a compressed description of an extremely creative, complex and wide ranging vision. It is the vision of Wole Soyinka, whose principal concern seems always to have been a series of mental and spiritual gulfs that exist, not only between the characters and forces of his plays, but also in Soyinka's real world, a world which is often far too selfish and insensitive to truth and artistic endeavor. Before plotting and exploring these divisions, it may be helpful to first take note of some general truths concerning Soyinka. This will enhance later efforts at analyzing specifics.

First of all, in terms of biographical information, it should suffice to say that Soyinka was born in 1934 of Yoruba parents, in the Nigerian city of Abeokuta. Almost every study devoted in part or totally to Soyinka carries adequate biographical information. However, care should be exercised due to discrepancies.[1]

Soyinka is Yoruba in literary background as well as heritage. This in no way diminishes his mastery of western dramatic technique or his understanding of western culture and theatre practice.

Soyinka has fused a mastery of western dramatic technique with an overpowering concern for the spiritual and physical survival of the Yoruba in particular and mankind in general. The concern that Soyinka possesses for his own indigenous culture has not made him self-serving or caused his plays merely to reflect the status of one ethnic group. His extensive use of Yoruba culture (mythology, philosophy, music, dance), is never solely for local exotic flavoring to heighten the plays' appeal. Though many western productions have tended to overemphasize the exotic in Soyinka's plays, his special interpretation of these Yoruba particulars gives them a universal flavor which causes them to be of interest to all of Africa and the rest of the world.

For much of the past two decades there has been an understandable concern expressed in many of the writings and actions of African nations. That concern was for the effect of Colonialism and Neo-colonialism. It should not be surprising that most African political activities and artistic creations are, in some manner, reflections of this concern. In this, Soyinka and the other Yoruba playwrights discussed here are no different than other African artists of the last twenty years or so.

It is, however, extremely important that the preceding statement be kept in its proper perspective. In the past, and at present, far too many critics have been preoccupied with this "cultural conflict theme" to the virtual exclusion of all other ideas. Although Africans are concerned with the effects of Colonialism, they do have other things to say and many different ideas to express.

At this point we should consider a truth which tends to set Soyinka apart from many of his contemporaries. While refusing to separate his art from social and political criticism, Soyinka has a propensity for pointing out the weaknesses in his society no matter where they may exist. It was partially this tendency, along with Soyinka's overall view, that set him at odds with the negritudists.[2] Unlike many negritude extremists, Soyinka does not believe that modernization

and new ideas are necessarily evil. Being more than
simply a reporter of circumstance, he often suggests in
his plays possible cures for the weakness that he sees.
Soyinka stresses the need for making honest, educated
choices when analyzing the fallout of Colonialism. For
many Africans this transition from the values of
Colonialism to values that are more African is an almost
impossible journey. Soyinka is extremely sensitive to
this fact and has often used his plays to lessen the
number of obstacles. He is aware that there can be no
total return to the past. One hundred years of
Colonialism has made that impossible. [3] However, there
can be awareness and rejuvenation of a culture that has
been purposely trampled on.

The journey back from Colonialism constitutes the
first abyss or gulf to be plotted and explored. It is, of
course, impossible to plot the total effect of
Colonialism on the Yoruba. However, it is necessary to at
least outline the particular aspect of the problem which
has caused Soyinka so much concern.

With varying degrees of efficiency, Africa's
colonizers sought to replace whatever indigenous cultures
they found with European facsimiles. This policy was
applied throughout the continent. The degree of its
success may have varied from country to country but the
effects were similar throughout. A more detailed view of
the African's situation would have revealed a people
ashamed of their very existence. In several countries,
especially those colonized by the French, there were
official assimilation policies which all but wiped out
the indigenous cultures. [4] Even in countries without
such official policies the end results were almost the
same.

A personal description of the situation and its
effect in Nigeria is given by noted novelist Chinua
Achebe.

When I was a schoolboy, it was unheard of to stage Nigerian dances at any of our celebrations. We were told and we believed that our dances were heathen. The Christian and proper thing was for boys to drill with wooden swords and the girls to perform, of all things, maypole dances. Beautiful clay bowls and pots were only seen in the homes of the heathen. We civilized Christians used cheap enamel wares from Europe and Japan; instead of water-pots we carried kerosene tins. In fact to say that a product was Ibo-made was to brand it with the utmost inferiority. When a people have reached this point in their loss of faith in themselves, their detractors need do no more; they have their point.[5]

It was in this state of despair and confusion that Soyinka saw his people (and to some degree himself) standing on the edge of an abyss with little knowledge of how to cross and even less understanding about where to start.

Even the approach of independence in the late fifties and the euphoria created by its promises were not enough to cloud Soyinka's mind to the pitfalls which lay ahead. Soyinka's concern for this transitional journey has become stronger as his plays have matured. Validation of his concerns and proof of his prophesies can be seen in the history of Nigeria since its independence in 1960.[6]

The second abyss over which Soyinka has attempted to build bridges exists in a somewhat more natural and predictable state. This abyss is one of differing concepts and understandings that are expected to exist from culture to culture. It is easily aggravated and

widened when subjected to insensitive manipulation.
The division is, basically, a combination of
differences that exist between Western culture and Yoruba
culture. These are differences which exist regardless of
cultural conflict or compatibility.

If alien cultures were always scrutinized with
tolerance and objectivity, cultural differences would
seldom become cultural misunderstandings. There is,
unfortunately, too much intolerance, a great deal of
cultural denial due to ignorance and contempt and, in
some instances, overzealous patronizing which can be just
as harmful as unwarranted negativism.

As stated in the introduction it is not necessary
for the western producer of Yoruba drama to be a
social-anthropologist. However, some familiarity with
Soyinka's thoughts on cultural differences may be helpful
when approaching the production of his plays and the
plays of the other playwrights. Soyinka believes that the
major cause of the conflict which he often sees existing
between Yoruba and western culture can be traced to basic
cultural outlooks instead of obvious surface differences.
While discussing drama and the African world-view,
Soyinka made the following comparison between European
and African drama as forms of representation.

The difference which we are seeking to define
between European and African drama as one of
man's formal representations of experience is
not simply a difference of style or form, nor
is it confined to drama alone. It is
representative of the essential differences
between two world views, a difference between
one culture whose very artifacts are evidence
of a cohesive understanding of irreducible
truths and another, whose creative impulses are
directed by period dialectics. [7]

These different world views can be reconciled without undue confrontation. To bridge this abyss, according to Soyinka, there is a "simple route to a common humanity made possible by the virtues of complementarity common in all cultures." [8]

The third abyss to be bridged is a metaphysical one which requires a certain recognition if not total understanding. It constitutes an extremely important belief for the Yoruba and its effects are often seen in Soyinka's plays. To over simplify, this traditional belief asserts that in the life, or reality, of the Yoruba there exist manifestations of the ancestral (past) and the unborn (future). [9] The concept of eternity for the Yoruba is represented by their deities. These manifestations are so interwoven into the life of the Yoruba that there is less distance between them and the realization of their beliefs, than exists in some other cultures.[10] For Soyinka and the Yoruba, these manifestations are proof of the belief that the distances which exist between man and these other states of being have increased over the years that stretch from the primal past. The rites of passage from one state to the other (e.g. birth, death) are extremely important. Soyinka points out that importance when he states:

This gulf is what must be constantly diminished by the sacrifices, the rituals, the ceremonies of appeasement to those cosmic powers that lie guardian to the gulf. Spiritually, the primordial disquiet of the Yoruba psyche may be expressed as the existence in the collective memory of a primal severance in transitional ether, whose first effective defiance is symbolized in the myth of the gods' growth which had sealed off reunion with man. For they were coming down, not simply to be acknowledged but to be re-united with human essence. [11]

The desire for transition into a spiritual reunion between man and the gods is, in the mind of Soyinka, the source of Yoruba tragedy.

> Tragedy, in Yoruba traditional drama, is the anguish of this severance, the fragmentation of essence from self. Its music is the stricken cry of man's blind soul as he flounders in the void and crashes through a deep abyss of a-spiritually and cosmic rejection...It is necessary to emphasize that the gods were coming down to be reunited with man, for this tragedy could not be, the anguish of severance would not attain such tragic proportions, if the gods' position on earth (i.e. in man's conception) was to be one of divine remoteness.[12]

Fashioning a bridge over this third abyss is undoubtedly, at times, a personal and private endeavor. It seems to reveal an urgency not present in the task of judging cultural values or searching for tolerance.

The primary consideration, however, in analyzing and producing the works of Soyinka is to simply be aware of possible minor obstacles.

THE DRAMAS

Analysis of Soyinka's work will include observation of and commentary on dramatic technique and script composition. Scripts will be viewed from the standpoint of mythological make-up and their unique artistic and literary tendencies.

Soyinka's plays have been categorized in several ways by various scholarly studies. These categories have proven to be more or less valid depending upon the scholar's point of view. [13] Since the primary aim of this study is demystification and the eventual production of the plays, new criteria must be used for play selection. The criteria used here sought to select the plays that, first of all, lend themselves to practical western production techniques. Though Soyinka's overall technique is often heavily western, it does not necessarily follow that his plays can be produced without concern for modifications. An example is the description of a Nigerian production of DEATH AND THE KING'S HORSEMAN given by Shola Olaoye. [14] Olaoye states that "virtually the entire population of a Yoruba village was used in the play to properly realize the effect of Olunde's funeral procession." Had the play's entire production been dependent on such a massive collection of humanity, its production outside of Nigeria would have been very difficult at the least. Secondly, the content of the plays selected had to hold a promise of interest for westerners. The thoughts and ideas could not be so immersed in indigenous expressions and practice as to render them totally obscure to outsiders. The third criterion eliminated those dramatic works which were primarily intended for mediums other than the stage. In the name of efficiency I have further chosen to eliminate plays that are from non-African sources with non-African core-content.

As stated in the introduction, these are the same criteria that are being used to select all of the plays being discussed. The nine plays discussed in this chapter will vary in their degree of sophistication and mystification. They will be discussed chronologically according to their approximate dates of composition and publication. Plays other than the nine chosen will be mentioned but only as instruments of clarification.

THE SWAMP DWELLERS

First produced in 1959, THE SWAMP DWELLERS may well be Soyinka's earliest play, written in 1957 or 1958. [15] It is a well thought-out play which provides certain clues to the major concerns and ideas which are to be found in virtually all of the dramatic works of Soyinka.

PLOT OVERVIEW

THE SWAMP DWELLERS is a one-act play which takes place in a delta village somewhere in Nigeria. Certain references in the play suggest that the area is the eastern part of the Niger delta in southern Nigeria. [16] The story concerns Igwezu, a young man who has left his village to find a better life in the city. He returns home a failure, only to discover that his land and crops have been destroyed by floods. Completely disillusioned, Igwezu begins to question his existence in what appears to be a totally hostile world. Unable to find comfort or solace in his village or in the city, he condemns both his traditional beliefs and what he considers the false promises of modernization. He finally leaves his home and his family with no clear view of his future.

THEMATIC CONTENT

THE SWAMP DWELLERS offers several themes and ideas that could be emphasized during production. The choice of how many or how few, of course, belongs to the director. The objective here, however, is to identify and plot the most significant possibilities.

The most obvious conflict in the play concerns the values of the young and new versus the traditional and

old. Igwezu challenges the teachings of his traditional
religion (the worship of the Serpent) and the actions of
its chief priest, the Kadiye. It has been Igwezu's
custom, as well as that of the other villagers, to make
sacrifices to the Serpent in order to insure an adequate
harvest and a decent level of existence free from flood
and the ravages of the swamp. From the beginning of the
play it appears that such has not been the case. The best
land has always been reserved for the Serpent, and it is
to remain untouched no matter what the hardship of the
villagers. This particular practice is spoken of to a
blind beggar by Igwezu's father, Makuri.

> The land that we till and live on has been ours
> from the beginning of time. The bounds are
> marked by ageless iroko trees that have lived
> since the birth of the Serpent, since the birth
> of the world, since the start of time itself.
> What is ours is ours. But what belongs to the
> Serpent may never be taken away from him. [17]

The climatic conflict comes when Igwezu, a barber
like his father, prepares to shave the Kadiye. While
threatening the priest with a razor, Igwezu vents his
iconoclastic anger at the fat, well-fed priest of the
Serpent. Here Soyinka is questioning the validity of
sacrifice and the honesty of the priesthood.

The play further brings into question the family
values held by Igwezu's parents. Igwezu's mother, Alu, is
certain that her other son, Awuchike, is dead because she
has heard nothing from him since he left for the city ten
years ago. Igwezu rudely shatters her beliefs when he
states that not only is his twin brother alive, but very
wealthy. He also informs them that he lost his new wife
to Awuchike while in the city. It seems that the

materialism and wealth of the city is much stronger than the homespun values of Igwezu's village. When asked by his parents if Awuchike remembers them or his home, Igwezu replies, "Awuchike is dead to you and to this house. Let us not raise his ghost." [18]

It seems that Soyinka wanted particular attention paid to the ideas of Igwezu. To accomplish this end he has the blind beggar treat Igwezu not as a failure but as a masterful and wise young man. He offers to become Igwezu's servant. He further agrees with the religious misgivings expressed by Igwezu and joins him as a fellow iconoclast.

For the director who wishes to view the play symbolically, it might prove fruitful if he is somewhat familiar with pre-independence Nigeria. [19] Such an approach may require more in depth study and analysis.

Finally, the play may be viewed as a treatise on maturity. Igwezu is beginning to recognize certain unpleasant truths concerning his traditional values that were, perhaps, hidden because of his youthful naivete.

THE TECHNICAL VIEW

THE SWAMP DWELLERS is a rather simple play that adheres to practically all of the classical criteria including unity of time. It contains none of the unconventional techniques that we will see in Soyinka's later plays.

When reading the opening stage directions it appears that film technique would be more appropriate. However, there are many staging possibilities which can assure that the needed atmosphere of darkness and isolation is provided.

The play has been criticized as being weak because it is highly derivative. Aaccording to Gerald Moore, Soyinka owes a great deal to Synge for the character of

the Blind Beggar, and Oyin Ogunba cites the obvious
biblical symbols such as the serpent and the swamp
landscape which is reminiscenct of the "primeval void of
the Genesis story." [20] I am not convinced that this
factor need be of any great concern. The manner in which
Soyinka has arranged and developed these elements works
quite well. An excellent example is the development of
the beggar. The height of the character's development can
be seen when he explains his reasons for leaving home. [21]

An item of greater concern may be found in the area
of character development. Soyinka has Igwezu attack the
Kadiye with such abandon that it appears at times to be
the ranting of a spoiled child. Add to this the Kadiye's
inability to protect himself or his faith verbally and we
have a questionable conflict. There is, in reality, no
one to voice the opposing view. The Kadiye runs away and
we are left with only the view of Igwezu and the beggar
fully expounded. In addition, Igwezu seems to hold
himself completely blameless for any of his misfortunes.
This child-like attitude, at times, elicits pity rather
than admiration.

The only mythical mystery in THE SWAMP DWELLERS is a
reference which Igwezu makes to his "mask."

> Igwezu: Can you see my mask, priest? Is it of
> this village?
> Kadiye: Yes.
> Igwezu: Was the wood grown in this village?
> KADIYE: YES.
> Igwezu: Does it sing with the rest? Cry with
> the rest? Does it till the swamps with the rest
> of the tribe? [22]

It is often the practice, in Yoruba religious
tradition, to divine a boy, at birth or later, as

belonging to a certain cult or group. The boy or young man is then socialized into the group, after having a wooden mask carved for him. When he is old enough he dances at celebrations as a masquerader with his mask group. [23] Igwezu may be referring to both the wooden mask and to his position within his group and village. He wonders why he is treated so unjustly by the Serpent to whom he has always paid proper homage.

THE LION AND THE JEWEL

Written in 1958 and rewritten in 1962, THE LION AND THE JEWEL is not one of Soyinka's most mature plays but it is, perhaps, his most charming play. It is so charming that at times it seems a shame to weight it with serious thought or weighty ideas. With the possible exception of THE TRIALS OF BROTHER JERO, it may be Soyinka's most produced play. It is a wonderfully comical critique of stiff traditionalism and superficial cultural progress, but not necessarily of any conflict between the two. It reveals hints of the ingenious talents that will be more fully displayed in Soyinka's later plays.

PLOT OVERVIEW

THE LION AND THE JEWEL is the story of a lovely young village girl, Sidi. She finds herself being wooed by both the village school master, a young man named Lakunle, and the village chief, a sixty-two year old leader named Baroka. Lakunle is the most educated person in the village. He stresses the importance of western modernization. Baroka, on the other hand, is a traditionalist who appears to want no part of progress. The choice between them is not as easy as it appears on the surface. Quirks in Sidi's character, added to the ethnocentricities of Lakunle and Baroka create a very interesting situation with a surprising outcome. The fact that neither Baroka nor Lakunle are really what they appear to be provides for a very entertaining story.

THEMATIC CONTENT

An overwhelming temptation, when analyzing THE LION AND THE JEWEL, is to over-emphasize the surface implications of a serious social conflict. If the play is viewed exclusively from this standpoint, much of its appeal will be lost.

There appears to be a conflict between the modern ideas of Lakunle and the traditional ones of Baroka. However, when viewed closely, the conflict diminishes considerably.

Much of the criticism of THE LION AND THE JEWEL has been based solely on this point. Perhaps the fact that it was often performed on the same bill as THE SWAMP DWELLERS influenced the critics. Whatever the reasons, the charm and light-heartedness is almost never mentioned. The play is called "a battle of ancient and modern" by Ronald Bryden. [24] Oladele Taiwo states that the play "compares the old and new order in Nigerian society" and "the struggle between progress and tradition." [25] Referring to the play as "bad," Mazisi Kunene called Soyinka's treatment of this conflict "superficial" and "shallow." [26] This mid-sixties criticism is challenged by later criticisms such as those of Gerald Moore who sees "a play of exceptional charm and dexterity," [27] and Oyin Ogunba who believes "the real achievement of THE LION AND THE JEWEL is the overall gaiety of the play." [28]

A close look at the make-up of the three main characters may hold some clues as to what the play comments on. Lakunle certainly represents the attractions of modernization. He wishes to convert his village into a modern metropolis like Lagos or Ibadan. He is familiar with the social amenities such as proper ballroom and cocktail party conduct. He wishes to discard traditional practices such as polygamy, the paying of bride-price, and the use of clay pots. Despite Lakunle's professed love of progress, it seems that he is more in love with its practice than with its practical benefits. He is unable to separate its substance from mere trappings. He gives the same credence to tea drinking and beauty contests as he does the need for roads and factories. [29] Perhaps his desire to erase the traditional is due, in part, to the fact that he is neither strong, handsome nor very popular in his village. And he may believe that modernization would improve his personal lot. He wishes desperately to marry Sidi, and she is willing to marry him if only he would pay the bride-price. His refusal may be due more to his inability to do so than his contempt for a "savage, barbaric, out-dated custom." In other words, Lakunle is not the crusading savior totally consumed with his view of the future. He is as ordinary as anyone else in his village and, at times, quite likeable.

Baroka is accused by Lakunle of preventing progress simply because it might interfere with the leader's authority and comfort. This assertion is contradicted by the fact that Baroka has built a school in which Lakunle teaches and has also allowed his servants to become unionized. What Baroka seems to fear most is not change itself but a too rapid one which might needlessly destroy worthwhile values.

Above all else Baroka is cunning, with the ability to manipulate those around him. A case in point is his masterful seduction of Sidi. He overcomes her opposition by appealing to her vanity and by presenting himself as a caring and strong individual. Sidi sees him in a much more pleasing light than Lakunle.

Sidi plays the role of village beauty quite well. She is aware of her youth and beauty. She feels that it brings her even more distinction than Baroka's position brings him. A great deal of this self-worship is due to the picture of her that was placed in a magazine by a visiting photographer. Some of her vanity, though, was present long before the photographer came. Her readiness to ridicule what she thinks is her impotent chief and suitor attest to that fact. There is no way to be certain if her final acceptance of Baroka as her husband is due to her professed self-interest or to Baroka's cunning. Perhaps it is a little of both.

Soyinka's major concern may have been the play itself, much as an academic or intellectual exercise. There is no real animosity between any of the characters. Both Lakunle and Baroka are jokers and, at times, enjoy their relationship. None of the characters nor any of the ideas receive a total commitment. Of course the references to modern and traditional culture should not be ignored. They should be kept in perspective.

THE TECHNICAL VIEW

The outstanding technical aspect of THE LION AND THE JEWEL is Soyinka's use of mimed action to represent past actions. This flash-back technique is quite effective. Each of the play's three sections includes dance and music that is much more complex than the simple drumming found in THE SWAMP DWELLERS. These mimed flash-backs give the play a much wider scope. This particular technique will appear often in Soyinka's later works.

A possible item of concern for the producer is the playwright's use of verse for the three main characters. There is a sense of stiffness in some of the verse speeches. An example is Sidi's speech after seeing the stamp machine. The machine is supposed to print stamps that bear her likeness. Her verbal reaction is, "I have never seen the like." [30] These strange-sounding lines also appear in the speech of Baroka. One such line is "What an ill-tempered man I daily grow towards." [31]

In opposition is the speech of Sadiku, Baroka's senior wife. Her speech is written in prose and is free of the odd-sounding lines mentioned above.

Finally, it may be a good idea to pay special attention to the character of Lakunle. There should be a near even balance between his seriousness and his foolery. To allow an imbalance in either direction could harm the production. The importance of this balance is pointed out by Gerald Moore when he writes of Femi Euba's perfect portrayal of Lakunle which provided just the right amount of satire and sympathy. [32]

Soyinka has provided translations of the Yoruba songs used in THE LION AND THE JEWEL. The items left untranslated are the prisoner's pub songs, the titles of which are found in the stage directions for the second mime. The first of the two song titles listed is "Nijo Itoro." The song, which translates as:

> Whenever I have threepence
> whenever I have sixpence
> It is always palm-wine.
> I would have been married by now
> But for the palm-wine gourd. [33]

There are also references to two Yoruba gods. There is a reference to Ogun, the hunter, god of iron, steel, and the road. All craftsmen and anyone who works with tools owe homage to Ogun. Also mentioned is the god Sango, the god of wrath and lightning. According to oral tradition Sango was at one time human. He dispenses the vengeance and retribution of Olodumare, the supreme god.[34]

THE TRIALS OF BROTHER JERO

If the only yardstick for measuring a play's success were its popularity based on frequency of production, then THE TRIALS OF BROTHER JERO would be Soyinka's most successful play. It addresses the need for fulfillment and guidance that all humanity must face at some time. It also satirizes the gullibility that is often a part of unquestioned loyalty and the temptation to corrupt and abuse religious teachings.

THE TRIALS OF BROTHER JERO will require far less space for analysis than some of Soyinka's longer plays. It should also generate less fear in the minds of western producers than many of Soyinka's other plays. Because of its simplicity it can provide a great deal of enjoyment and satisfaction for smaller theatre groups.

PLOT OVERVIEW

The play concerns a beach prophet named Jeroboam who conducts his divine profession as a business. He is an intelligent and resourceful rogue who has the ability to charm his way into or out of almost any situation. He is served by a rather slow, dim-witted follower named Chume. Chume is married to Amope, a shrew, who is a constant aggravation to him. Amope, however, is wise enough to see through the deceptive veil of Jero. The play recounts a single day in the life of the prophet. It reveals through Jero's eyes, the conditions that existed on Lagos' Bar Beach during a period of religious transition and upheaval in Nigeria. [35]

THEMATIC CONTENT

The play reveals in Jero a frank, straightforward charlatan who is quite honest with the audience. He readily reveals that the practice of his profession is based largely on his economic needs. The audience sees his strengths and weaknesses and despite his lack of genuine charity, he is victorious throughout. Soyinka appears to be of the opinion that people who are themselves dishonest, stupid, or greedy, deserve whatever leadership they get. The director should remember that the play addresses the trials of Jero, not the trials of those used by him. Intelligence and cleverness demand respect even if that respect is a bit questionable. This is especially true in the face of greed and stupidity. Jero does some things that should be considered contemptible. He has dispossessed his old master and teacher and he is purposely deceiving his chief follower, Chume. He is also avoiding payment of his debts to Amope. Jero appears to be something of a lecher and ends the play by having Chume confined as a raving lunatic. Through all of this Soyinka manages to keep Jero far less tarnished than seems appropriate.

The play could be seen as a warning to those who, for whatever reasons, are susceptible to the type of leadership offered by Jero. Soyinka does not condemn Chume. He presents him rather sympathetically. However, there is no way for Chume to avoid his fate. If it is impossible for him to be more alert and inquisitive, then his deception is to be expected. The play generates more pity for Chume than it does anger at Jero for his treatment of Chume.

The deceptiveness of Jero is not confined to the poor or uneducated. A great part of his success is due to

36

social conditions. The Member of Parliament is an
excellent example of the social ills. His desire for a
ministerial post overrides his common sense and makes him
a prime target for Jero. Notice also the strange values
of the community. The people care more for high-sounding
names than they do for substantive leadership.

The merchandising of religion by both merchant and
consumer is an important concern, not only among the
Yoruba, but wherever religion exists.

THE TECHNICAL VIEW

In view of the play's length it is not surprising
that the characters are, more or less, stock types. There
is the shrew, the dull comical servant and the dishonest
prophet. In spite of this Soyinka manages to keep the
characters fresh and interesting. He even manages to keep
the interest alive when presenting actions that the
audience already expects. Jero tells the audience on
several occasions of his intentions. The execution of
those intentions is always more satisfying than the
expectations.

The play's pacing depends almost totally on Jero.
While speaking to the audience, he introduces the play
and moves it along in the same manner.

Soyinka makes good use of lighting technique and
stage arrangement. Well-timed blackouts and spotlighted
stage areas are essential in a play with a number of
settings and quick pacing.

THE TRIALS OF BROTHER JERO provides the first use of
pidgin English that we have seen in Soyinka's plays.
There is no problem in understanding its meaning as may
be the case in later plays. There are, however, parts of
Chume's pidgin that don't quite work. The failures are
due to a mixing of pidgin and standard English. An
example is:

Tell our wives not to give us trouble. And give
us money to have a happy home. Give us money to
satisfy our daily necessities. Make you no
forget those of us who dey struggle daily.
Those who be clerk today, make them Chief Clerk
tomorrow. Those who are messenger today, make
them Senior Service tomorrow. [36]

In addition to this awkward mixture special
attention should be given to scene five where there is a
mime by the Member of Parliament. He mimes a speech that
he is rehearsing for delivery in parliament. It should be
done in an exaggerated manner in order to achieve the
scene's full effect.

Chume's use of pidgin English and Jero's
introduction of nonsense words are the only instances in
the play which might cause concern. The terms "Abraka"
and "Hebra" have no real meaning. They are introduced
into the chant by Jero to demonstrate how easily Chume is
led. [37]

Two key terms used in Chume's pidgin speech are "na"
which means "it (he, she) is" and "make you" which means
"please." [38] The rest of the script should present few,
if any, problems.

THE STRONG BREED

With THE STRONG BREED Soyinka brings to the stage
many of the technical, literary, and philosophical ideas
that he will continue to use throughout his career. It
is a short play which is very concentrated and dynamic.
Soyinka has already proven that he has an outstanding
command of comic technique. He now proves that he is
extremely adept at dealing with serious drama. This
tragic side of Soyinka's art will pervade his remaining
plays.

PLOT OVERVIEW

THE STRONG BREED concerns a young man, Eman, who is living as a stranger in a town where he has worked as a dispenser for almost a year. The play opens with a great deal of foreboding as Eman's sweetheart, Summa, tries desperately to get him to leave town. She refuses to be specific about why she wants him to leave. It is clear, however, that as a native of the town she possesses certain knowledge that Eman is not aware of. Despite Summa's pleading, Eman does not seem overly concerned. In fact, by showing so little concern, he appears to invite whatever it is that Summa fears.

We learn later that Summa's fear is due to the approach of the town's annual New Year's Eve ritual, which requires that a carrier or scapegoat be chosen to bear the town's sins for the past year. The carrier is always a stranger. Since Eman is a stranger, Summa's apprehension is understandable.

There is only one other stranger in town. He is an idiot boy named Ifada, who has already been chosen by the town leaders. When Eman is finally made aware of the choice, he is upset. He is fond of Ifada who is, in addition to Summa, the only other person that Eman considers a friend. We also learn that, ironically, Eman is a hereditary carrier. It has been the practice among Eman's people to utilize hereditary carriers who voluntarily suffer through the ritual. The forcing of an unwilling stranger into the role of scapegoat is offensive to Eman. Eman's disgust causes him to insult the festival chief Jaguna, who happens to be Summa's father. It quickly becomes apparent that this insult, plus a challenge from Summa's father, will cause Eman to trade places with Ifada.

The remainder of the play deals with Eman's

treatment by the townspeople, his reaction to that treatment, and his eventual death.

THEMATIC CONTENT

In Eman, the play presents a character who is worthy of respect and admiration despite the struggle within him. In previous plays we have seen Soyinka reject traditional figures. The Kadiye in THE SWAMP DWELLERS is one example of that rejection. Approval of Eman demonstrates that disapproval of particular characters and their ideas does not mean blanket disapproval of traditional views.

The self-sacrifice that is part of the scapegoat tradition provides, in Soyinka's mind, a desirable model for those who wish to aid their community. Just like Eman, this savior would be asked to sacrifice without regard for his personal survival. The failure of Eman to remove the sin and guilt from the town was due, in part, to his contempt. It was also due to the town's corruption and indifference to sorrow and pain. It is quite clear that the town does not deserve a strong carrier able to bear the suffering demanded. We must assume that Eman voluntarily trades places with Ifada in order to save his life. The boy would probably have never survived the ordeal. It appears that the only good to come from Eman's death is a closer relationship between Ifada and Summa.

Before any production is attempted it would be wise to address the question of why Eman tries to escape from Jaguna and the others during the ritual. Was it a conscious effort to disrupt their festival and deny the selfish and cowardly populace their ritual cleansing? Was it Eman's fear that he would not be able to undergo the suffering as his father had done? Jaguna's accomplice, Oroge, may provide a hint of an answer.

Jaguna: Why then did he refuse to listen? Did he think he was coming to sit down at a feast. He had not even gone through one compound before he bolted. Did he think he was taken round to the people to be blessed? A woman, that is all he is.

Oroge: No, no. He took the beating well enough. I think he is the kind who would let himself be beaten from night till dawn and not utter a sound. He would let himself be stoned until he dropped dead.

Jaguna: Then what made him run like a coward?

Oroge: I don't know. I don't really know. It is a night of curses Jaguna. It is not many unprepared minds will remain unhinged under the load.[39]

It is impossible to avoid the idea of predestination in THE STRONG BREED. If we accept the play's contention, we accept the idea that the individual cannot possibly escape his destiny. In the first flash-back scene between Eman and his deceased father it becomes clear that Eman has not been at ease with his lot in life. He has searched for years trying to find some answers. All that he learns during his years of searching seems totally useless when, at the grave of his wife Omae, he realizes that the peace of mind that he sought was always at home with her and his people. Even though the death of his wife seems to drive him further away from home and deeper into himself, he cannot escape his fate as a carrier.

Some producers of THE STRONG BREED may be intrigued by the play's statement concerning guilt. Eman feels guilty because of Omae's death and his evasion of his hereditary duties. The community suffers from a collective guilt. There is only one way that we can rid ourselves of guilt, be it individual or collective, and that is to face it. We must atone for our guilt or run the risk of worsening our situation as did the townspeople. It is quite clear that the use of carriers, be they willing or not, is ineffective at truly eliminating guilt. Note the conversation of Jaguna and Oroge concerning the death of Eman.

Jaguna: Then it is a sorry world to live in. We did it for them. It was all for their own common good. What did it benefit me if the man lived or died. But did you see them? One and all they looked up at the man and words died in their throats.
Oroge: It was no common sight.
Jaguna: Women could not have behaved so shamefully. One by one they crept off like sick dogs. Not one could raise a curse.
Oroge: It was not only him they fled. Do you see how unattended we are?
Jaguna: There are those who will pay for this night's work!
Oroge: Ay, let us go home. 40

THE TECHNICAL VIEW

The smooth presentation of any production will depend on the careful staging of the flash-back scenes. As was the case with THE SWAMP DWELLERS, this play makes a strong demand on stage technique. There are three flash-back scenes, all of which require special attention. The first scene, between Eman and his father, presents an event that takes place shortly before the father's death. The problem here has to do with recognition. The director must be sure that the audience knows that the character talking to the old man is a younger Eman and that he and the character watching the scene are one and the same.

Flash-back number two is much more explicit and easier to deal with. It concerns Eman and Omae at the age of sixteen. The flash-back technique will be more familiar to the audience by this time. This scene concentrates more on the link between present and past.

The third scene is more complicated than the first two. It is difficult to tell what is past and what is present. The flash-back begins with the death of Omae and its effect on Eman. At this point it is interrupted by a short scene set in the present. When the flash-back resumes it deals not with Eman and Omae but with Eman and his father.

It is important to preserve the highly charged atmosphere of THE STRONG BREED. Soyinka provides the tension by having constant confrontations in each scene, even the flash-backs.

Once the tradition of the carrier is addressed there is little else to obscure any of the play's meanings. Since many westerners will be familiar with the idea based on the life of Christ, only an optional search for detailed facts might be deemed necessary. [41]

THE ROAD

Long considered the premier playwright in Africa, Soyinka took his place among the best playwrights of the contemporary era with THE ROAD, written in 1964. He demonstrates in this play an impressive maturity and refinement of technique. THE ROAD is praised by Soyinka's admirers and those who have, at times, been his harshest critics. [42] The play's ideas are complex and often leave the reader confounded on his first attempt. Continued study, however, will reveal a work of great richness, intriguing beauty, and a haunting idealogy which lends itself to the same unending scrutiny and analysis that we associate with the best of dramatic works.

For quite some time THE ROAD was considered Soyinka's best play. There are later plays which compare favorably.

PLOT OVERVIEW

THE ROAD is set in what Soyinka has labeled the "Aksident Store." It is a makeshift roadside store which sells auto parts that have been gleaned from road accidents. The store's proprietor is the Professor, a mysterious figure clad in Victorian attire. The store's manager, recently hired by the Professor, is Kotonu, a former lorry driver who has decided to quit the road. Kotonu's tout, Samson, does not want him to work in the Professor's store. Samson questions the morality of profiting from the misfortune of others. In addition to the characters listed above there is Murano, a palm-wine tapster who also works for the Professor and who is apparently a mute. Other characters who frequent the Aksident store are Salubi, a would-be driver and chauffeur, and Say Tokyo Kid, a truck driver and sometimes hired thug. Occasionally the store is visited by Chief-in-town, a corrupt politician and Particulars Joe, a rather untrustworthy policeman. There are also a number of thugs and layabouts.

The play revolves around what the Professor calls his search for "the word." He is intentionally vague about his search and its meaning. We learn later that the Professor is trying to uncover the essence of death. He wishes to violate the shroud of secrecy that veils the transition from life into whatever lies beyond. To accomplish his goal, it appears that the Professor is not above causing the deaths of others by removing crucial road signs. He rushes to each new accident, not only to keep his Aksident Store supplied, but to also search for some clue that will reveal the "word" to him.

Like the Professor, Kotonu is also searching for answers. His search, however, seems more human than the cold metaphysical groping of the Professor. Kotonu is finding it hard to accept the death that he sees constantly on the road. He finds the traditional justifications unacceptable, yet he can find no new doctrine to rid him of his concerns.

Samson thinks that Kotonu is over reacting and that the traditional beliefs and practices should be enough. For him the answer is simple. Ogun is the drivers' patron and god of the road. They need only pay proper homage to Ogun and they will have no worries. A closer examination of the facts, however, proves Samson's contention to be unfounded. Part of Samson's reason for wanting Kotonu to continue driving is so Samson can continue being a tout. It is also revealed that Samson had tried desperately to become a driver but did not have the ability. He then paid for Kotonu's training and driver's license. He is partly fulfilling his desire to drive through Kotonu.

The Professor's talent for forgery keeps Salubi at the store. He has been trying for some time to get the Professor to forge him a driver's license. Even with a license Salubi is not likely to have much success as a driver. Like Samson he does not possess the ability.

The other characters have various reasons for patronizing the Professor's store, not the least of which is the Professor's habit of serving them palm-wine in the evenings. It is an activity which he refers to as communion. Chief-in-town stops by whenever he needs bodyguards or enforcers for one of his political rallies. Say Tokyo Kid is his principal employee and Chief-in-town often pays him and the other layabouts with hemp.

According to Particulars Joe, his frequent visits have to do with police investigations. He makes it quite clear that he is not above accepting bribes.

Soyinka weaves these motivational concerns, both petty and profound, into an engaging story that reveals the universal need that man has for some type of order and meaning in his existence.

THEMATIC CONTENT

The most popular item for analysis in THE ROAD has always been the Professor and his search for the word. The Professor has been referred to as a hero, a magician and as a parody. His search for the word has been called a search for the "indestructible energy of God" by one critic and a "mockery" and a "farce" by another. [43]

The temptation to search for themes within the characters themselves is understandable. Yet, an overall view of the play must not be overlooked. The Professor is one of Soyinka's most intriguing characters. An analysis of his character is certainly called for, but not to the exclusion of the rest of the play. The director must decide if the Professor is to be taken seriously or not. Is he no more than a parody of intellectualism or is he a profound thinker with lessons for us all? Whatever the position taken by the director, it should be based on the script and not on previous criticism.

THE ROAD is mostly a play about death and how the various characters react to it. None of them seem to accept its inevitability. Not even the Professor in his diligently intellectual search seems willing to face death himself. His preoccupation with death leads him to sleep in the graveyard but not to risk being its victim. The Professor, like Faust, is seeking knowledge and is willing to risk offending the gods in order to find it. What is not clear is his motive. Is it an admirable desire to understand a great mystery or merely a false exercise designed to hide immoral profiteering? The Professor's cold indifference may suggest the latter. However, plotting the Professor's motivation will not be an easy task. His character is often ambiguous. This contributes to the interpretive confusion while, at the same time, adding to his appeal. The Professor was, at one time, a Christian lay-reader. After a dispute with his bishop the Professor leaves the Christian church apparently disillusioned with its approach to the essence of immorality. It is at this point that he undertakes his present course of inquiry and experimentation with Murano, who, while dancing as an egungun masquerader, is hit by Kotonu's lorry. When struck, Murano is in his Agemo or transitional phase. The accident suspended him between life and death and provided the Professor with the perfect opportunity for penetrating that transitional essence.

Samson is very traditional in his view of death. He is predictably afraid of it and seeks to avoid it with the traditional sacrifices. Because of his belief in tradition he insists on Kotonu's running over a dog now and then to satisfy Ogun's hunger. He is afraid that Ogun will demand human sacrifice, and that he might be that sacrifice.

Ironically, the loud, westernized Say Tokyo Kid is as traditional as Samson. He relies on a talisman to protect him from death and the spirits he believes to be in the lumber that he transports.

Kotonu, unlike the Professor, is very disturbed by the cold indifference of death on the road. He is certainly afraid of dying, yet, he tries to accept its inevitability. Kotonu's search is guided by a desire for true understanding. This attitude places him beyond the blind acceptance of tradition that we see in Samson and

Say Tokyo Kid as well as the psychic mysticism of the Professor.

A second theme, one that we have seen in Soyinka before, is his concern with guilt and atonement. Easiest to detect is the guilt of Kotonu. He feels that he escaped death at the horrible bridge accident because of the chance intervention of another lorry. He is extremely confused about the masked dancer that he hit with his lorry. He is certain that he killed the masquerader, but the body disappears. His guilt and confusion cause him to quit the road. He seems to be waiting for punishment.

Samson and Say Tokyo Kid deal with guilt in pretty much the same manner that they dealt with death. Samson has followed traditional practices much like Igwezu in THE SWAMP DWELLERS and seems to have had no experience traumatic enough to shatter his complacency.

Things are a bit different for Say Tokyo Kid. His role as leader of the thugs is becoming an unsettling experience. It may be this uncertainty which causes his rash actions at the end of the play.

A casual interpretation might seem to indicate that the Professor is not capable of feeling guilt. His attitude toward death and the fact that he may possibly have caused several accidents seems to indicate that his strong intellectual pursuits have replaced any humanity that he might have once possessed. However, when consideration is given to the Professor's more subtle reactions, the preceding interpretation seems inadequate. A case in point is the Professor's reaction to Salubi's threat of suicide when the Professor refuses to forge him a license. The Professor is quite upset because he believes that to speak of death (the word) in such a manner is to invoke its dreadful power.

Kotonu is undoubtedly the play's most admirable character. The Professor, however, remains its most interesting and dramatic.

THE TECHNICAL VIEW

THE ROAD is very economical in setting and structure. The play is divided into two sections, the actions of which take place in a single setting. The play's time covers approximately twelve hours. The setting, which consists of the Aksident Store and a church yard, is divided by a fence. The setting lends itself well to proscenium staging. The impression of one area intruding on the other might be lost if the setting were non-proscenium.

There is a weakness in the play's structure caused by the Professor. He is a brilliant creation with which Soyinka must take an inordinate amount of time. The time spent making the Professor and his search credible causes the rest of the play to suffer a bit. Whatever else happens in the play seems secondary to the Professor and his actions. As the professor seeks to confuse the rest of the characters with the mystery surrounding the "word," he may also be confusing the audience and obscuring what is supposed to be the play's central thought. The problem, fortunately, does not appear as great on stage as it does on the written page. Casting may hold the perfect answer. The director must be sure that all of his actors are strong, not just the Professor. It would be a mistake for the director to expect to find definitive answers in the Professor's search. I am not certain that there are any concrete answers to be found in a production or a scholarly analysis regardless of their depth.

Soyinka abandons the use of verse that we saw

earlier in THE LION AND THE JEWEL. There is less
dependency on words and more on the intensity of the
situation. The play's speech ranges from the "correct
English" of the Professor and Kotonu, through the pidgin
of Samson and Salubi, to the Americanized slang of Say
Tokyo Kid and Particulars Joe. There should be no great
problem with the language. Soyinka provides a glossary of
pidgin terms.

Samson's habit of switching from standard English
to pidgin may cause some confusion. An example is his
conversation with Salubi at the opening of the play.

> Salubi: Go mind you own business you
> jobless tout.
> Samson: Me a jobless tout? May I ask
> what you are?
> Salubi: A uniformed private
> driver--temporary enemploy.
> Samson: God almighty! You dey like
> monkey wey stoway in sailor suit.
> Salubi: Na common jealousy dey do
> you. I know I not get job, but I get
> uniform. [4]4

A possible explanation might be Soyinka's double
responsibility for authenticity and understanding.

In THE ROAD we find that Soyinka has refined the
use of one of his favorite devices, the flash-back. He
provides, in the character of Samson, an excellent mimic
who has the ability to relay past events with amazing
clarity.

This role-playing technique is much less
troublesome than the flash-backs we saw in THE STRONG
BREED. The best example of this new technique is Samson's
re-enactment of the church duel between the Professor and
the bishop.

Special note should be taken of the music used in THE ROAD. Chanting, drumming, and singing are used to reinforce many of the scenes. Such a scene involves Say Tokyo Kid's use of the drum to call his gang of thugs. The last scene, in which the Agemo dances, is also an important drumming scene. According to Dr. Oyin Ogunba:

> Agemo music is done with "apepe" percussion sticks and has a steady, fast beat which usually gets much faster with the increasing inebriation of the performers; it is a very appropriate symbolic indication of possession. [45]

The singing and chanting are also used to increase the intensity of the play's thought. The chanting of the layabouts is used to highlight Samson's role-playing scenes. Another scene worthy of note is the chanting scene in which the thugs go off to engage in some violent political activity for Chief-in-town. In their song the thugs sing of their power and willingness to crush all who oppose them.

Also there is the scene which contains Kokolori's dirge. The dirge serves to intensify our feeling that someone special has died. In the words of the song, "Death has sinned against us, A man among men is gone." [46]

Soyinka's use of music in this play gives the impression that music underlies all of the action and intensifies when necessary.

Fortunately for western producers Soyinka provides translations of both the chants and the pidgin English. He also provides an enlightening note at the beginning of the play which helps to explain the mask idiom as well as the search of the Professor. The poem ALAGEMO is also supposed to shed light on the meaning of the "word." A further discussion of the poem and the Professor is in order here.

The preface poem tells of a spirit, Alagemo, who is summoned from the bowels of the earth. He tells of a future that will be dominated by the spirit of mystery and death. Agemo symbolizes that spirit. It is a dark, incomprehensible spirit, one that can not be resisted. It is the essence of this spirit that the Professor seeks to uncover, a search that he pays for with his life. [47]

Soyinka's translations are quite adequate. However, there are several terms which can be explained further. In the translation of the thugs' war-chant the terms Oro and Esu appear. Oro is a fierce and mysterious Yoruba spirit of punishment. Esu is an equally fierce, emotional, mischief-mongering god. [48] There is also a term, "bolekaja," used in the opening stage description that is translated as "mammy wagon." Soyinka is right in thinking that this term would be easily recognized. It does not, however, convey the fierce and reckless abandon with which these passenger vehicles are driven. The term "bolekaja" literally means "come down and fight." [49]

KONGI'S HARVEST

With KONGI'S HARVEST, Soyinka moves heavily into the realm of political satire. In none of his other plays are the thematic intentions so obvious. Unlike THE ROAD, KONGI'S HARVEST moves back to some of the more familiar techniques and devices that were seen in some of Soyinka's earlier plays. Considered an extremely topical play for the mid-sixties, it still carries a relevant message.

PLOT OVERVIEW

The play concerns what appears to be a newly independent African nation called Isma. There is a political struggle in Ismaland between the traditional monarch, Oba Danlola and a modernized intellectual dictator named Kongi.

As the play opens, it seems that the bulk of the power rest with Kongi. He has confined Danlola and several of his followers to a detention camp. The immediate conflict concerns the disposition of the season's New Yam. Traditionally, the New Yam is always presented to the Oba (king) who eats and blesses the yam harvest. Kongi feels that this ritual act of purification should now fall to him, since he is the country's new political leader. Realizing that many of his countrymen still believe in tradition, Kongi is careful not to be excessive. He plans to usurp Danlola's power but with the appearance of harmony.

As the play reaches the end of the prologue, entitled, "Hemlock," we are given the impression that the traditionalists may see signs of the end of their rule.

The play's first part is composed of a series of rapid scenes that alternate between Kongi's mountain retreat and a night club which is operated by Segi, former mistress of Kongi. She is now the consort of Daodu, a young man who happens to be the nephew of Danlola and heir to the throne.

The action follows the movement of Kongi's Organizing Secretary who moves back and forth between the retreat and the night club. In the first scene at the retreat we are shown Kongi's Reformed Aweri Fraternity. It is a group of intellectuals who are supposed to function much as the president's cabinet. It is soon clear that the only thing they are good at is useless disputation. The second scene takes place at the night club. Kongi's Secretary has come to ask the aid of Daodu in convincing the Oba to relinquish the honor of receiving the year's first yam. Surprisingly, Daodu seems willing to help. Segi, whose father is awaiting execution for his part in a plot against Kongi, rejects the Secretary and his proposal.

After several visits between the night club and the retreat, the Organizing Secretary finally gets a promise of aid from Daodu. Daodu's promise is contingent upon an earlier promise made by Kongi. The dictator has promised to release all of the Oba's followers who are awaiting execution. Daodu appears to have a plot of his own, but no details are given.

In the play's second part we find that Danlola, having agreed to give up the first yam, is now changing his mind. When Daodu trys to find out why, Danlola tells him that Kongi has issued a "dead or alive" order for one of the Oba's followers. The escapee happens to be Segi's father. In Danlola's opinion Kongi has broken his promise. With some difficulty Daodu convinces Danlola to attend the festival. He promises his uncle that there will be no need for regret. Daodu again implies that he has a plan. Disheartened, Danlola attends the festival and honors his promise to give the first yam to Kongi. At the moment that he does so, gunfire is heard off stage. The apparent reason is an attempt by Segi's father on the life of Kongi. We learn that the attempt has failed and that Segi's father is dead. The failure seems to strengthen Kongi's resolve while demoralizing Daodu and his mysterious plan. The only one still capable of action is Segi. She leaves and after a few minutes, returns with a copper salver which is passed to Kongi. When he lifts the lid he finds the head of Segi's father. Kongi is horrified and speechless. The festival celebrants run away as a blackout ends the play.

The 1967 published version of KONGI'S HARVEST

contained what might be considered an epilogue. During
this final section, entitled, "Hangover," we see the
Organizing Secretary and Oba Danlola fleeing for the
border. It appears that after the upheaval at the
festival neither of them is safe in Ismaland.

THEMATIC CONTENT

In discussing THE ROAD the director was warned
against an extensive analysis of characters which might
cause the overall meaning of the play to be ignored. That
advice should be reversed when analyzing KONGI'S HARVEST.
The characters in KONGI'S HARVEST are so clearly
personifications of ideas that they demand close
scrutiny. Unlike THE ROAD's Professor, there is very
little that is intended to be mysterious about them. The
play lends itself to several broad interpretations.
However, the shaping and clarification of ideas come with
study of the characters, not the play's situation.

The most obvious theme has to do with the conflict
between traditional rule and contemporary political
power. Since some type of force is the only means by
which a non-traditional political power can quickly
establish itself, the conflict is rather predictable. If
this were the play's only thought it would not be worthy
of a great deal of interest. Fortunately the characters
provide other possibilities and, perhaps, the key to the
author's intent.

Soyinka's satire exposes the greed and other
follies found in his main characters. Through them he
offers a rather profound thought on politics. Soyinka
stated that" KONGI'S HARVEST is about dictatorships and
so on." [50] There can be no doubt that Kongi is a dictator
and, at times, he appears quite ruthless. However, there
are some missing characteristics which we might have
expected to be present. For instance, Kongi does not seem

to be corrupt or evil in the sense that he is totally without concern for the welfare of his people. He has not enslaved or murdered large numbers of them nor does he seem very interested in great personal wealth. His problem seems to be his preoccupation with theory and intellectualism. It is as if he is unaware of a great deal that is real and pertinent.

When we first meet Danlola, we are shown a monarch with dignity and the welfare of his subjects at heart. He is an old man who seems to be fighting valiantly for traditional values against great odds. At this point he is an admirable character worthy of our respect. Later, in the second part, Soyinks shows us a different side of Danlola. He has lost some of his dignity and becomes a rather foul-mouthed bully who continuously insults his servant. His stature is further diminished by his acceptance of Daodu's abusiveness. Perhaps these are the understandable reactions of a king who knows that he must surrender his power and position. However, it is difficult to accept his running for the border in the epilogue.

Daodu has the potential for being the most respected and effective character in the entire play. His position as heir to the throne, his education and apparent understanding of politics, would seem to make him the perfect choice as savior of Ismaland. Despite all this, Daodu is weak and inept. Part of this ineptness is due to Daodu's relationship with Segi. Her actions are much stronger and more precise than Daodu's. A perfect example is Daodu's lack of action after the death of Segi's father. He seems lost until Segi gives him instruction. We cannot be certain if Daodu really had a plan to deal with Kongi. An optimistic view of Daodu's character might see him as one day being strong enough to deal with his country's dilemma.

The Organizing Secretary is the only obviously

corrupt character in the play. Despite his being a crook, he is not vicious or inhuman. His character is largely the stereotypical idea of a political "yes-man." His commitment to Kongi may have been only a superficial one since the Secretary flees the country with Danlola.

It is difficult to label the character of Segi. What is known of her is, to a great extent, based upon what is reported about her rather than upon her actions. We can see her control over Daodu and her bold actions during the yam festival. It is difficult to determine, however, if she is a brave patriot or a vindictive reactionary.

What KONGI'S HARVEST presents is a trio of main characters who are all deficient in one area or another. Danlola's chief interest seems to be himself. Kongi appears blind to reality and Daodu, as of yet, is not mature enough to make any significant contribution. The only reasonable explanation for this is that Soyinka intended that we see politics as a dead end. The problems of society often seem meaningless in the realm of politics.

THE TECHNICAL VIEW

In the writing of KONGI'S HARVEST Soyinka seems more concerned with subject matter than dramaturgy. When compared to THE ROAD it seems underdeveloped.

The play's first shortcoming is the lack of background information. There is little or no information provided about Isma's recent history. This lack of information is much more of a handicap in the west than in Nigeria.

There are also instances at which the play's action is slowed unnecessarily. For instance, there is little real need for the scene with the photographers. The play leaves unfulfilled the desire to see more of Kongi and

Segi. They were both worthy characters who were under dramatized.

The weakest point of all is the undisclosed plot of Daodu. A great deal of expectation is allowed to flatten when the plot seems to simply disappear at the play's end.

Only a few brief points remain to be clarified in order to assure a reasonable degree of understanding. In the dirge sung by Danlola during the prologue, the Oba sings of delving with the left foot during his dance. For the Yoruba the left foot is negative. According to Oyin Ogunba:

> Thus if a man leaves his house early in the morning to go to work and, five or ten yards away, he knocks his left foot against a stone, he may decide that it is a bad omen, return to the house and wait a few minutes before starting out again. [51]

There is also mentioned another Yoruba deity who we have not met heretofore. He is referred to in the opening dirge as the god "Whose hands of chalk have formed the cripple and the human bat of day." [52] The god is Obatala, the supreme divinity of Yorubaland. It is said that Obatala springs directly from Olodumare the supreme force. Obatala is the sculptor divinity.

> He is the sculptor divinity who has been given the prerogative to create as he chooses, so that he makes man of shapely or deformed features. The hunchback, the cripple, the albino, are regarded to be special marks of his prerogative, either signifying his displeasure at the breach of some tabu, or to show that he could do as he likes. [53]

The discussion of KONGI'S HARVEST can not be closed without mentioning the individual upon whom the character of Kongi is supposedly based. The first president of the Republic of Ghana was Dr. Kwame Nkrumah. Nkrumah is reported to have had many of the same characteristics as Kongi. Kongi has a Carpenters' Brigade while Nkrumah set up a paramilitary corps called the Builders' Brigade. Nkrumah was one of the first African leaders to use, like Kongi, preventive detention. He was also a staunch intellectual who sought to establish a new African philosophy called Conscientism. A more detailed study of Nkrumah will provide the director with some general background information on the political situation in Ghana during the late fifties and early sixties as well as possible insight into the character of Kongi.

MADMEN AND SPECIALISTS

The first play published by Soyinka following his more than two year imprisonment was MADMEN AND SPECIALISTS. With its 1971 publication we see a greater pessimism in Soyinka that ever before. Gone are the social saviors we have seen in earlier plays. Always flawed to some degree, characters such as Igwezu, Eman, Kotonu and Daodu have been replaced by a young man far more vicious than Kongi. The cynicism that we see in MADMEN AND SPECIALISTS is not all the result of Soyinka's personal incarceration. Recent events in Nigeria and other parts of Africa tend to justify Soyinka's pessimistic outlook. The regime of Idi Amin is but one example.

Whatever his motivation, MADMEN AND SPECIALISTS is one of Soyinka's most disciplined plays.

PLOT OVERVIEW

The play opens with four mendicants engaged in a game of dice. They are playing, not for money, but for their remaining limbs and organs. They are Aafaa, a spastic, a cripple, a blind man, and Goyi, who, because of a brace, must remain in a permanent stooping position. As they play they speak about the "theory of the truth," which seems to make no sense at all.

The mendicants stop their game with the entrance of Si Bero and start to beg for money. Si Bero is in charge of the nearby clinic and she invites the mendicants to come and work for the money they want.

At this point we meet Iya Agba and Iya Mate who live in a hut in the Bero family compound. The two old women are there at Si Bero's request to teach her herbalism, a form of medicine based on the use of herbs.[54]

Dr. Bero, Si bero's brother, arrives and is warmly greeted by his sister. He, however, is very cold toward his sister and the old women. The brother and sister are now joined by the local priest as Dr. Bero's coldness continues. We learn from their conversation that, like his father, Bero is a medical doctor who has been away serving as a specialist in the war zone. We further learn that Bero's father, after receiving a letter from his son, decided to join the war effort. The father, referred to as "Old Man," was quite upset with the level of killing reported by his son.

Since that time Si Bero had heard nothing of him and is anxious to know of the Old Man's whereabouts. Her brother tells her of how the Old Man's preoccupation with cannibalism had caused him to serve the officers human flesh for dinner. He was then assigned to rehabilitate war victims. In the meanwhile Dr. Bero had been transferred to the post of senior intelligence officer.

To his sister's shock and amazement Bero states that the Old Man has been home for some time hidden in the basement surgery. He has been watched by the mendicants who are Bero's spys.

It is revealed later that Bero has had his father declared insane and is torturing him trying to learn the meaning of a new philosophy formulated by the Old Man called "As." It seems that the philosophy of As was taught to the mendicants during what was supposed to have been their period of rehabilitation. They know the teachings of As but not its meaning.

Bero's earlier rudeness has upset the two old women in the compound, and they have decided, despite Si Bero's pleading, to punish him for his lack of respect. They claim to be earth mothers and say that they will call down the wrath of the gods on Bero. Iya Agba is about to do this, by throwing a pot of glowing embers into the store, when Bero appears with gun in hand. Before he can take any action against her he is distracted by loud noises coming from his basement surgery. The action shifts to the basement and we see the Old Man, aided by the other mendicants, about to operate on the cripple. Bero enters and shoots the Old Man as he raises his scalpel. At that moment the embers are flung into the store causing the house to catch fire. As the house burns the mendicants cheerfully chant their favorite song as the lights suddenly black out and the play ends.

THEMATIC CONTENT

MADMEN AND SPECIALISTS is a play steeped in despair and hopelessness. Society, symbolized by the mendicants, is portrayed as blind, crippled, and insane. There are no young saviors here. It seems that they have provided only a false hope of salvation and that Soyinka is abandoning them. Dr. Bero, the obvious candidate for the role of savior, has allowed the power of his position to make him vile and heartless. Society's traditional element, symbolized by the Old Man, becomes totally fatalistic. The Old Man creates a new philosophy which is of no more use than past philosophies. Perhaps destruction by the very primal forces that created him is mankind's ultimate destiny.

There are several possible themes that are present but by themselves are too small in scope to justify a play of this stature. There is, of course, the theme of family relationship, which is concentrated in the conflict between Bero and his father. In addition, there is the possible religious theme of primal purity versus modern corruption.

The most profitable theme to investigate is concerned with the idea of social change. It seems that mankind is truly unable to deal with social change in any rational manner. Perhaps the changes come too quickly. There is nothing new in the idea of war and death. Yet, when it comes for what seems to be no reason, the establishment is unable to provide any type of meaningful leadership or vision. It, like the Old Man, allows its humanity to flounder in a fit of nihilistic cannibalism. The younger members of society, the educated and idealistic, allow themselves to become materialistic androids. They are fascinated with the power and promise of their technical abilities which leaves them devoid of any humanity.

Perhaps the effects of social shocks, like a sudden military takeover or the side effects brought on by rapid technical advances, are never to be adequately analyzed and dealt with. Soyinka may be simply presenting society as it exists with no suggestions for how it should be.

There is a great temptation to see Si Bero as a hope for the future. She is the only uncorrupted character and seems to be in line to inherit at least some of the knowledge and power possessed by Iya Agba and Iya Mate. She has withstood a great deal of adversity and disillusionment. Yet, at the end of the play, with her world burning around her, she seems to stand in its midst untouched.

THE TECHNICAL VIEW

MADMEN AND SPECIALISTS is a very well thought out play. Almost every aspect of the play is properly proportioned.

One of the most pleasing aspects of the play is the stage setting. In past plays Soyinka has offered rich descriptions and meaningful stage decorations, but the settings were usually of one level with actions that moved, more or less, in a straight line.

In MADMEN AND SPECIALISTS the setting is divided into three separate levels which enhances the play's action. It is almost imperative that the basement surgery be on the lowest level with the clinic at stage level and the hut for the old women on a level above the stage floor. Closer study will reveal that the scenes are divided equally between each level with the final scene taking place on all levels practically simultaneously. It is also interesting to note which scenes take place on which level.

On the highest level, that of the earth mothers, are staged very short scenes which are concerned mostly with the supernatural air of the old women. At the middle, or stage level, are performed the scenes which are less intense and provide mostly background or superficial information. The most intense and meaningful scenes are played on the lowest level. These are the scenes in which Soyinka shows us man's inhumanity and the hopelessness of his condition.

By having the last scene take place on all three
levels at once, the scene's destructive finality is
greatly enhanced.

Despite the fact that MADMEN AND SPECIALISTS is a
very disciplined play, there are a few points which might
cause confusion. The true nature of Iya Agba and Iya Mate
is, at times, a bit obscure. A literal translation of the
name Lya Agba is "big mother" and often refers to a
grandmother or the oldest woman in the family or
neighborhood. Iya Mate means "mother Mate" (Mate is a
proper name). [55] They state that they are earth mothers.
They may be thought of as witches or "aje." The term in
Yoruba describes one "who can influence lives for good or
ill." [56] Si Bero knows that the old women have unusual
power. It is for this reason that she asks their aid in
the safe return of her father and brother. She, however,
is not learning witchcraft from them.

The action of the final scene and the stage
directions for it may also be confusing. According to the
stage directions:

> [He raises the scalpel in a motion for
> incision. Bero fires. The old man spins, falls
> face upwards on the table as the cripple slides
> to the ground from under him. A momentary
> freeze on stage. Then Si Bero rushes from the
> Old Women towards the surgery. Instantly Iya
> Agba hurls the embers into the store and thick
> smoke belches out from the doorway gradually
> filling the stage. Both women walk calmly away
> as Si Bero reappears in the door way of the
> surgery. The mendicants turn to look at her,
> break gleefully into their favorite song. The
> Old Women walk past their hut, stop at the spot
> where the mendicants were first seen and look
> back toward the surgery. The song stops in

mid-word   and   the   lights   snap   out
simultaneously.] [57]

The problem comes with the word "store." Does
Soyinka mean the house/clinic or the area where the herbs
are left to dry? According to Dr. Joseph O. Okpaku the
word should be "stove" instead of store. [58] The compound
stove would resemble a barbecue pit. Whatever the
destination of the embers, the act of their being flung
is a ritual one. It is through this act that the old
women call down the wrath of the gods on Bero.

JERO'S METAMORPHOSIS

In 1973 Soyinka published a sequel to THE TRIALS OF
BROTHER JERO entitled JERO'S METAMORPHOSIS. The two
principal characters, Jero and Chume, are the only
characters retained form the first play. As the title
implies Brother Jero has changed a good deal. Chume,
however, is the same. The change in Jero is indicative of
the change that we saw in Soyinka during the analysis of
MADMEN AND SPECIALISTS.

PLOT OVERVIEW

The opening stage directions of JERO'S
METAMORPHOSIS contain the first hint of change, not only
in Jero, but also in the political environment in which
Jero exists. According to the directions Jero's personal
situation has obviously improved. He now occupies a
"modest whitewashed room" equipped with a surplus file
cabinet and an "ancient, but functioning" typewriter.
There is on one wall of the room a picture of a
"uniformed figure at a battery of microphones." It seems
that Jero's homeland is no longer governed by civilian
politicians. [59]

The first scene reveals Jero in the act of dictating a letter to Rebecca, an attractive young woman who works as Jero's secretary. The letter is an invitation to the other beach prophets to meet with Jero concerning a matter of great importance to them all. They are being threatened with the loss of their livelihoods.

It is clear that Rebecca is quite taken with Jero. She is his convert as well as his employee. It seems that when Rebecca came to Jero she brought with her a certain file in which Jero has a great interest. Jero is aware of his effect on Rebecca, and he is pleased with his ability to control her.

Outside of his office Jero is approached by Ananias, a fellow beach divine and an ex-convict who seems to be still practicing his earlier profession as a hired thug. He has come to inform Jero of a decision by the City Council to rid the beach of all prophets and their followers. Jero is aware of the development and plans to make it the subject of the meeting that he has just called.

We become aware at this point that Jero has lost none of the cunning and resourcefulness that he possessed in THE TRAILS OF BROTHER JERO. A demonstration of Jero's ability comes after his authority and position as leader of the prophets is challenged by Ananias. Jero reveals the he has certain information which if made public could return Ananias to jail. After Jero proves that the information is genuine, Ananias is humbled and becomes Jero's follower.

Also in the first scene the Chief Executive Officer of the Tourist Board of the City Council and his clerk come to retrieve the file that was given to Jero by Rebecca. They waited until Jero had gone before approaching Rebecca. Through the ensuing conversation we learn that Rebecca was once Miss Denton, Confidential Secretary to the Chief Eviction Officer. She had come with him to notify Jero of his impending eviction when she was converted and has been devoted to Jero ever since. Physically overwhelmed by the religious fervor of Rebecca and Ananias, the Chief Executive Officer and his clerk flee without retrieving the file.

In scene two we finally learn of Chume and the nature of his predicament since he was committed to an asylum in THE TRIALS OF BROTHER JERO. The Salvation Army, needing a trumpeter for their band, rescued Chume from the asylum and made him not only their trumpeter but also gave him the rank of corporal as well. Jero has not seen Chume since he was committed, but he proves during their first meeting that he has not lost his control over him. Chume is predictably upset because of what Jero has done to him, but he is quickly won over by Jero's smooth tongue. Jero tells Chume that, by the will of God, he is now a prophet also and that he will receive a further promotion at tonight's meeting.

Scene three brings the culmination of Jero's plan to deal with the threaten evictions. He intends to unite all of the prophets under his leadership and to consolidate the various religions into a single religion. The new religious organization is to be known as The Church of the Apostolic Salvation Army of the Lord. According to the secret file, the only religious organization exempt from the purge was to have been the Salvation Army. Jero plans to capture this religious monopoly for his new organization instead. To accomplish this he blackmails the Chief Executive Officer. It seems that the file also contained certain information pertaining to the illegal awarding of contracts for construction of a new national amphitheatre to be built on Bar Beach. The Chief Executive Officer, having little choice, signs an agreement which gives Jero's new organization the monopoly on religious activity.

Having earlier assigned rank to some of his

followers, Jero now gives Chume his final promotion as "Brigadier Joshua." He watches as his army of followers march out of sight. Jero then replaces the picture of the uniformed individual with a larger picture of himself in his new CASA uniform.

THEMATIC CONTENT

Many of the same ideas that were discussed in connection with THE TRAILS OF BROTHER JERO also apply to JERO'S METAMORPHOSIS. THE TRIALS OF BROTHER JERO was a simple, amusing play that could be done principally for fun. JERO'S METAMORPHOSIS is much less so. It is comical, yet the humor is sardonic, and the intent is satirical.

Jero is no longer the happy-go-lucky rogue with only the simplest of problems. The situation now demands that he deal with a serious threat that not only he but the rest of his society is threatened by. He responds with the only weapons at his disposal. He calls upon his wit and cunning.

There is something frighteningly familiar about Jero's opponents and their methods of operation. The practice of political deception fostered by back room deals and self-serving corruption is not alien in any culture.

This corruption is what Soyinka is anxious to uncover in JERO'S METAMORPHOSIS. There was nothing in THE TRIALS OF BROTHER JERO to match it. Certainly the change in Jero himself demands some thought. The metamorphosis has caused Jero to be much more cynical. We are, at times, not certain if Jero's actions are now based on survival or greed. Has he fallen in love with the very type of power and corruption that he is fighting? Is he practicing blackmail because it is the only way of reaching the agents of the establishment? Is there a desire in Jero to replace the present leadership with himself? His promise to the CEO not to interfere in secular affairs, coupled with his lines at the end of the play, would seem to indicate an affirmative answer to most of these questions. We can do little more than compare his present attitude and condition to those which existed in the past. The fact that a substantial amount of time is unaccounted for between the two plays cannot be overlooked. There has been a war and a change of government. Is the new harsher Jero the product of a natural evolutionary process or is Jero simply responding in the only manner that he can to his present circumstances? Whatever the opinion of the director, care should be taken to avoid the use of character extremes, especially if both plays are done on the same bill.

THE TECHNICAL VIEW

Like THE TRIALS OF BROTHER JERO, the characters in JERO'S METAMORPHOSIS are also stock types. The plot of the later play is a bit more complex than the earlier one. This is perhaps a reflection of Soyinka's ever increasing maturity as a playwright. Gone are the numerous soliloquies which held together the plot of THE TRIALS OF BROTHER JERO. JERO'S METAMORPHOSIS is a much more intense play. It has few scene changes and fewer scene locations. There is less pidgin spoken by Chume in the latter play, and it is less confusing.

JERO'S METAMORPHOSIS causes few interpretive concerns. It may be helpful to mention Bar Beach and the part it plays. The government of Lagos had developed the habit of staging public executions on the beach. This practice was intended as a deterrent to lawlessness among the populace. The executions, however, became something of an entertainment and began to attract large crowds of people. The area leaders saw in this an opportunity for profitable enterprise. The proposed National Amphitheatre was intended to house these executions.

DEATH AND THE KING'S HORSEMAN

First published in 1975, DEATH AND THE KING'S HORSEMAN contains the first non-African characters that we have seen so far in Soyinka's plays. This factor, despite the play's preliminary notes, seems to have been the focal point for many of the play's earlier critics. In his preliminary notes Soyinka warns against the "clash of cultures" theme that has been so overworked by critics of African literature. Written in 1973-74 while Soyinka was at Churchill College in England, the play is a fascinating portrayal of self-sacrifice and communal rejuvenation. It is more than the story of a ritual, it is a reenactment.

PLOT OVERVIEW

The play opens with the appearance of Elesin Oba (Horseman of the King) and his Praise-Singer, Olohun-iyo. Elesin is anxious to reach the market place so that he can avail himself of the preferential treatment that he knows he will receive from the women there. While approaching the market the Praise-Singer speaks of the importance of Elesin's forthcoming death and spiritual journey to join their king. Elesin assures him that he looks forward to the honor of joining his king and will not shrink from his duty.

After reaching the market the men are greeted by Iyaloja, the mother of the market, and the rest of the women who clothe Elesin in the finest cloths.

While accepting the admiration of the women, Elesin notices a beautiful young woman. He has never seen her before but it is clear that he wants her. Since Elesin is their chief and since he is approaching the all important moment when his death will allow him and his king to enter the realm of their ancestors, he is given the young woman as his bride. This is done despite the fact she has been betrothed to Iyaloja's son.

Scene two introduces the District Officer, Simon Pilkings and his wife Jane. As the scene opens they are preparing for a costume ball being held at the Resident's Palace. Pilkings and his wife are costumed in the sacred attire of the Egungun Cult. It seems that the outfits were confiscated during an Egungun activity which was supposedly causing trouble.

The Egungun attire upsets Sgt. Amusa who comes to tell Pilkings that Elesin plans to "commit death." It is unclear to Pilkings if Amusa means murder so he summons his Christian houseboy, Joseph. Joseph informs Pilkings that Amusa was referring to the fact that it is Elesin's duty to commit ritual suicide so that he can accompany the king, who died last month, on his journey to heaven. Not wanting to miss the ball, Pilkings sends a note to Amusa telling him to prevent the suicide and to detain Elesin in the District Officer's residence.

Amusa's attempt to carry out Pilkings' instructions is foiled by the market women who ridicule him and his two accomplices and force them to leave the market. Saved from interruption, Elesin emerges from his wedding hut and prepares to carry out the ritual that will mean his death.

Meanwhile, a new character, Olunde, appears at the costume ball searching for Pilkings. Olunde, the eldest son of Elesin, has been away studying medicine. He has returned for the funeral of his father which he knows was to follow the death of their king by one month. He wishes to avoid any trouble that may come as a result of Pilkings or anyone interfering with his father's ceremonies. He has no idea that Pilkings left the ball earlier to do just that. Before the scene ends Elesin is brought on stage in handcuffs. When he sees Olunde he is overwhelmed by shame and is chided by his son.

It becomes evident during scene five that Pilkings' intervention has caused a great upheaval among Elesin's people. Trying to avoid further trouble Pilkings allows Iyaloja to visit Elesin, who is now shackled and locked in a cell. Elesin is verbally punished by Iyaloja for not fulfilling his obligation to them and his king. She then informs him that Olunde has saved the honor of his house. The body of Olunde is brought in by the women. Pilkings rejects Elesin's request to be let out of his cell long enough to whisper a parting message to his son. Elesin, unable to cope with the situation, strangles himself with the chain of his handcuffs. The play ends as Elesin's young bride closes his eyes in death.

THEMATIC CONTENT

Just as he did with THE ROAD, Soyinka provides preliminary notes which should serve as a guide to his thematic intent. The notes for DEATH AND THE KING'S HORSEMAN are more demonstrative than they were for THE ROAD. Soyinka makes it very clear that his principal interest is not the "clash of cultures" theme. The colonial intervention, as destructive as it is, is not the primary concern. According to Soyinka:

The Colonial Factor is an incident, a catalytic incident merely. The confrontation in the play is largely metaphysical, contained in the human vehicle which is Elesin and the universe of the Yoruba mind--the world of the living, the dead and the unborn, and the numinous passage which links all: transition. DEATH AND THE KING'S HORSEMAN can be fully realized only through an evocation of music from the abyss of transition. [60]

These are virtually the same ideas discussed earlier in the chapter and referred to as the third abyss.

DEATH AND THE KING'S HORSEMAN contains several of the same concerns that we first saw in THE STRONG BREED. Again we see a situation wherein the welfare of the community is dependent upon the self-sacrifice of an individual. Elesin, like Eman, is bound to the act of sacrifice by heredity and tradition. Unlike Eman, there is no conflict within Elesin. He gladly accepts his role and appears eager to fulfill his duty. The primary concern in DEATH AND THE KING'S HORSEMAN is not the heroic or tragic efforts of an individual but the essence of a tribal tradition. What we see are aspects of the personality of death itself. It is not the sacrilegious intrusion that the Professor represents in THE ROAD. The Professor's death is punishment. The death of Elesin was to have been an honorable act that would have insured the continued vitality of his people. Even after Elesin's moment of weakness and failure, the traditional debt will not be denied. Death wins what is due through Olunde. The passage is only temporarily interrupted.

The intrusion of Colonialism, in the person of Pilkings, is the primary reason for the tragedy that befalls Elesin. The Oba could have easily overcome his small personal weakness. The result of pilkings intervention is to be expected when one people presume to guide and govern with no real understanding or true sensitivity toward the governed.

One item which deserves attention is the uniqueness of Elesin's character. Elesin possesses both the humorous and the tragic. He appears to be the personification of Soyinka's statement concerning the process of transition.

Elesin does not question; he simply accepts. Unlike his predecessors, Danlola and Baroka in particular, Elesin seems totally free of complication. He admits his faults and weakness as easily as he points out his accomplishments. DEATH AND THE KING'S HORSEMAN comes closes to bridging the third abyss.

THE TECHNICAL VIEW

DEATH AND THE KING'S HORSEMAN uses song, dance and poetry to fashion a unique picture which tends to invite audience participation. These elements build in intensity until there is a harmonious mixture. It is what Soyinka means when he says "the movement of words is the very passage of music and the dance of images." [61]

The play becomes the ritual instead of a retelling or an exercise. There is very little in the script that is unnecessary. The humor, that might be frowned upon in traditional tragedy, seems natural and appropriate in DEATH AND THE KING'S HORSEMAN.

The play is not overly dependent on language. The dialogue seems a natural complement to the action. The play should be easy to stage due to the fact that Soyinka has successfully merged theme and technique.

The activity surrounding the ritual of the king's horseman should be easy to comprehend. There are two terms which might require a short comment.

The first term, Egungun, was mentioned in the section that dealt with THE ROAD. The discussion was, however, confined mostly to the Agemo phase. The Egungun is a secret cult which demonstrates the Yoruba belief in life after death and the belief that the dead can still communicate with the living. The Egungun:

> ...designates the spirit of the deceased with
> whom intercourse is held at the ancestral

shrine. It materializes in a robed figure which is designed specially to give the impression that the deceased is making a temporary reappearance on earth. This reappearance may be that of a specific ancestor. Where this is to be the case, a rite of "creating" the egungun takes place on the fortieth day after the burial; and after that the reappearance takes place periodically, once a year or more often.[62]

The second term, juju, appears in the same section of dialogue as does egungun and is defined by E. Bolaji Idowu in the following manner.

Another label which has been flung about indiscriminately is juju. The French must have thought that the cult objects of West Africa were no more than ridiculous playthings; for the word is said to be derived from the French jou-jou, which means "toy". It has, however, been employed extensively as a comprehensive expression which purports to convey all that is meant by religion in West Africa. [63]

DEATH AND THE KING'S HORSEMAN ends our discussion of Soyinka. However, the overwhelming dedication and sophistication that we see here, continues in OPERA WONYOSI and A PLAY OF GIANTS published in 1984.

NOTES

CHAPTER TWO

1
    Several sources list 1935 as the year of Soyinka's
birth. Two such studies are "The Traditional Elements of
the Yoruba Alarinjo Theatre in Wole Soyinka's Plays"
(p.x), by June Balistreri and "Introduction to West
African Literature" (p.78), by Oladele Taiwo. I have
accepted the year 1934 because it appears in studies that
were reviewed by Soyinka before being published.

2
    The philosophy of Negritude was founded by Leopold
Sedar Senghor in the mid-thirties. It advocated that art
should be judged not by its intrinsic value but by the
contribution it made toward the restoration of the
dignity of the African. Others, Soyinka among them,
disagreed. They felt that emphasis should be placed on
the universality of the beauty of a work of art and that
there should be a literary standard which is
internationally acceptable.

3
    Michael Crowder, A SHORT HISTORY OF NIGERIA (New
York: Frederick A. Praeger, 1962), pp. 134-68.

4
    Oladele Taiwo, AN INTRODUCTION TO WEST AFRICAN
LITERATURE (New Jersey: Nelson, 1967), pp. 48-49.

5
    Ibid., p. 49.

6
    Since Nigeria's independence in 1960, it has gone
through a civil war and no less than four forced changes
in the central government, the latest occurring in 1985.

7
    Wole Soyinka, MYTH, LITERATURE AND THE AFRICAN WORLD
(New York: Cambridge University Press, 1976), p. 38.

8
    Ibid., p. xii.

9
    Ibid., p. 148.

10
E. Bolaj Idowu, OLODUMARE: God in Yoruba Belief (London: longman, 1962), p. 5.

11
Soyinka, p. 144.

12
Ibid., p. 145.

13
The two most popular methods for categorizing Soyinka's plays have been, one, according to their perceptible maturity and two, according to their level of pessimism.

14
Personal interview with Shola Olaoye, Cultural Consultant for 1983, North Carolina Central University production of DEATH AND THE KING'S HORSEMAN, 10 November 1982.

15
Joseph O. Okpaku, "From Swamp Dwellers to Madmen and Specialists: The Drama of Wole Soyinka," Diss. Stanford Univ., 1978, p. 20.

16
Oyin Ogunba, THE MOVEMENT OF TRANSITION (Ibadan:Ibadan University Press, 1975), p. 24.

17
Soyinka, COLLECTED PLAYS I, p. 92.

18
Ibid., p. 104.

19
An excellent and concise study of pre-independence Nigeria can be found in Michael Crowder's A SHORT HISTORY OF NIGERIA.

20
Ogunba, p. 28.

21
Ibid., p. 31.

22
Soyinka, COLLECTED PLAYS I, p. 108.

23
Ogunba, p. 20.

24
Okpaku, p. 49.

25
Ibid., p. 50.

26
Ibid., p. 50.

27
Gerald Moore, WOLE SOYINKA (New York:Africana Publishing Corporation, 1971), p. 27.

28
Ogunba, p. 53.

29
Wole Soyinka, COLLECTED PLAYS II (New York: Oxford University Press, 1974), pp. 36-37.

30
Soyinka, COLLECTED PLAYS II, p. 50.

31
Ibid., p. 47.

32
Moore, p. 27.

33
Ogunba, pp. 44-45.

34
There are no likenesses or worship objects of Olodumare. It is impossible for man to totally comprehend his existence.

35
Beginning in the late 19th century groups of Africans, disgruntled with the missionary churches, formed their own churches called "Aladura." This process of synthesis continued through the 1950s and produced the situation that we see on Bar Beach. For more information see J.D.Y. Peel's, ALADURA: A Religious Movement Among the Yoruba (London: Oxford University Press, 1968).

36
Soyinka, COLLECTED PLAYS II, p. 160.

37
Ibid., p. 160.

38
Okpaku, p. 84.

39
Soyinka, COLLECTED PLAYS I, p. 132.

40
Ibid., P. 146.

41
For more detailed information see Robin Horton's article, "New Year in the Delta", NIGERIA MAGAZINE, no. 67, 1960, pp. 256-96.

42
Okpaku, p. 156.

43
Moore, p. 57.

44
Soyinka, COLLECTED PLAYS I, p. 152.

45
Ogunba, p. 156.

46
Soyinka, COLLECTED PLAYS I, p. 191.

47
Oyin Ogunba, "The Agemo Cult in Ijebuland," NIGERIA MAGAZINE, no. 86, 1965, pp. 176-86.

48
Idowu, p. 42.

49
Interview with Olaoye, 10 November 1982.

50
"Interview with Soyinka," SPEAR MAGAZINE, excerpts from CULTURAL EVENTS IN AFRICA, 18 May 1966, pp. 2-3.

51
Ogunba, p. 170.

52
Wole Soyinka, KONGI'S HARVEST (New York: Oxford university Press, 1967), p. 9.

53
Idowu, p. 71.

54
  Okpaku, p. 191.

55
  Ibid., p. 195.

56
  Ulli Beier, "Gelede Masks," ODU no. 4, 1956, p. 16-32.

57
  Soyinka COLLECTED PLAYS II,p. 276.

58
  Okpaku, p. 194.

59
  Soyinka, COLLECTED PLAYS II p. 175.

60
  Wole Soyinka, DEATH AND THE KING'S HORSEMAN (London: Eyre Methuen, 1975), p. 7.

61
  Soyinka, MYTH, p.141.

62
  Idowu, p. 193.

63
  Ibid., p. 2.

III

THE SEARCH FOR HISTORICAL TRUTH

OLA ROTIMI

Among Yoruba playwrights who write in English, Ola
Rotimi's prominence is second only to Wole Soyinka's. The
son of a Yoruba father and Ijaw mother, Rotimi was born
in 1938. In 1959 he began a six year period of education
in America which resulted in a Bachelor's degree from
Boston University in 1963 and a Master of Fine Arts
degree in playwrighting from Yale in 1966.

Rotimi's international reputation as a playwright is
based largely on an adaptation that is not included in
this study. The play, THE GODS ARE NOT TO BLAME, is a
reworking of Sophocles' OEDIPUS REX. The play was given
an African setting and concerns Yoruba royalty. There is
little significant difference in the story line.

Written in 1969 during the Nigerian civil war, the
play, according to Rotimi, is a reminder that Africa
should take responsibility for her failures as well as
her successes and not seek to blame the "political gods
of our age," namely Russia, America and China.[1] The play
is also a condemnation of what Rotimi refers to as
tribalism and ethnic distrust. It is Rotimi's opinion
that this distrust was the root cause of the civil war,
and he makes it the basic tragic flaw of the play's hero,
Odewale. [2]

Of Ola Rotimi's five published plays, two are in
accord with the criteria set out for this study. The two
remaining plays, apart from THE GODS ARE NOT TO BLAME,

present no difficulty in understanding and staging. They are OUR HUSBAND HAS GONE MAD AGAIN, a mildly satirical comedy written in 1966 at Yale and published in 1977 and HOLDING TALKS, a short absurdist drama published in 1979. The earlier play is a domestic comedy with political overtones. According to Rotimi the play "attempts to warn the Nigerian electorate to watch out for political charlatans of whom there are many in the land." [3] HOLDING TALKS is a satire on the senseless propensity that man has for employing useless dialogue and empty discourse in situations that require action.

The brief mention made of THE GODS ARE NOT TO BLAME provides a hint of Rotimi's major concern and his method of dealing with that concern. He feels that the key to peace and human survival lies in strong human affiliations. This is especially true of African nations in light of the continent's almost constant turmoil. To further this perceived need for selfless brotherhood, Rotimi has reverted to deeds of the past and attempts to use them as part of his contemplation of the future. His historical dramas also serve to re-educate many of Rotimi's countrymen in the events of a past that they have been taught to disregard. He emphasizes the truth and honor that is understood and cherished by people of all cultures.

Rotimi's belief in and appreciation of these lessons of the past can be seen in his appraisal of his own role as a dramatist. In 1972 Rotimi stated:

> I see my role as contributing to the better understanding of the Nigerian personality through appreciation of the sweat of our forbears. This appreciation might stimulate us, perhaps, toward evolving a better society, and thus vindicate our existence as worthy

successors   to   the   heritage   of   our
self-sacrificing forbears. [4]

THE DRAMAS

Being a good deal less prolific than Soyinka, Rotimi
has, of course, attracted less analysis and criticism.
Analysis of Rotimi's work will follow the same guidelines
set out in the Introduction. Several factors concerning
the work of Rotimi should be taken into consideration
before we embark on a detailed analysis of the plays.
Before 1969 when Rotimi's KURUNMI was first produced,
there was no African drama of this type or historical
magnitude written in English. Rotimi has a combination of
reasons for adopting this form. He believes that the use
of large casts, crowd scenes, and music and dance will
serve to establish a definite identity for African drama.
Rotimi has stated:

> Some of the characteristics of an African
> Theatre, I think, should be those that can be
> easily identified with African culture itself.
> Music is one, dance is another. Again, there
> is the use of crowds. Most African celebrations
> involve some amount of communal participation,
> and the use of crowds in a play is one way of
> establishing some definition of an African
> Theatre. But these cultural elements should not
> be gratuitously applied. I use them only where
> I think they can either emphasize the point
> being made or where they can heighten the
> dramatic effect. [5]

These artistic beliefs and dramatic techniques can also
be found in the works of other playwrights. Rotimi,

however, makes much more extensive use of them.

Rotimi also derives a great deal of pleasure from his historical epics. When asked about his ultimate artistic ambition he replied saying that he wanted to "write a full-length massiveness in music, dance and movement lasting two whole hours and a half directed by me, mobilizing a 500-man cast." [6]

KURUNMI

First produced at the University of Ile-Ife in 1969, KURUNMI is labeled by its author as "Nigeria's first historical drama." [7] It should be pointed out that the play is not an accurate reflection of historical text. It is a dramatization of certain historical events. The oral tradition is still quite prominent in Nigeria, and Rotimi relies on it quite heavily for his creative innovations. [8]

PLOT OVERVIEW

KURUNMI concerns a period of civil strife in the 19th century Yoruba Empire referred to as Oyo. Some background information is necessary here to insure that the events of the play are viewed in proper perspective.

Throughout the 18th century a great portion of western Nigeria and neighboring Dahomey came under the influence of the Oyo Yoruba and their ruler the Alafin. At the start of the 19th century there was a strong challenge to the power and authority of the Oyo Empire. A revolt in Ilorin, one of its northeastern cities, was aided by an old enemy of the Empire, the Fulani. The Empire saw its capital destroyed and was forced to consolidate its defenses further south. During this period of strife the Alafin charged the cities of Ibadan and Ijaiye with the defense of the Empire. In 1840 the

Ibadan defeated the Ilorin and halted the invasion of the
Empire by the Fulani. The ruler of the Ibadan was
appointed Basorum (Prime Minister) of Oyo and the ruler
of Ijaiye, a general named Kurunmi, was appointed
Are-Ona-Kakonfa (Generalissimo).

At this point in history we move ahead some 18 years
to 1858 and the opening of the play. According to Rotimi,
it was in this year that the Alafin, being close to
death, asked that the Crown Prince, Adelu, be made the
new Alafin. This request was contrary to Oyo law and
tradition. It was the custom that upon the death of the
Alafin the Crown Prince was to commit suicide. The
Ibadan supported the request of the dying Alafin while
Kurunmi and the Ijaiye opposed it.

As scene one opens we see the citizens of Ijaiye
preparing for a feast. This jubilant mood is shattered by
the entrance of Kurunmi who is visibly upset. He tells
the people of the Alafin's request and informs them that
he considers it perverse and disgraceful. Scene one ends
with a visit from the rulers of Ibadan and Ede who try to
convince Kurunmi that he should change with the times and
accede to the wishes of the Alafin. Kurunmi refuses even
to consider the request. He insults the new Alafin by
refusing to attend his coronation. This forces a
confrontation in which the new Alafin offers Kurunmi a
choice of peaceful acceptance or war. Kurunmi immediately
chooses war without any regard for the wishes or opinions
of his followers. He holds to his decision even in the
face of some dissatisfaction on the part of his best
warriors and a good deal of pleading from the white
missionary, Rev. Mann.

The Ibadan decide to ally themselves with the Alafin
because they fear the power of Kurunmi and are not sure
if Kurunmi desires to conquer them also. The alliance of
Ibadan and the Alafin prove to be too much even for
Kurunmi. He is forced to ally himself with the Egba from

the city of Abeokuta, a long time enemy of the Ibadan. The Egba generals have no talent for strategy. Kurunmi, against his better judgement, leaves the choice of battle site to them. The Egbas chose to cross the River Ose and meet the enemy on their own ground. Knowing this to be a disastrous mistake, Kurunmi has no choice but to accompany the Egba in this final battle.

As feared, the Egba and Ijaiye are defeated. Kurunmi learns of the deaths of his five sons and in a state of total despair, commits suicide as the play ends. [9]

THEMATIC CONTENT

The central concern in KURUNMI is tradition. Both the idea of tradition and the concern for its observance is embodied in Kurunmi. His defense of and respect for tradition is stated early in the play as he relates the Alafin's shocking request to his followers.

My people, we too have tradition.
This is what makes us men.
This is what makes us...people, distinct from mud.
Why, the pride of bees is in the honeycomb.
The pride of the weaver bird
shows in the skillful design of its nest.
And where stands the pride of the monkey?
Is it not in his knowledge of the secrets on treetops?
The pride of man, my people,
is in his tradition -
something to learn from for the peace of his present:
something to learn from for the advance of his tomorrow.[10]

It is quite clear that Kurunmi sees in tradition the source of truth that has guided and protected his people from the time of their beginning.

As their spiritual leader, the Alafin should honor tradition above all else. His attempt at altering the royal succession to the throne is not for the benefit of his people. We can only assume that the requested alteration holds some personal gain for his family. This fact in part justifies Kurunmi's violent opposition even when the kings of Ede and Ibadan are asking him to accept the change as a sign of the changing times. There is a danger that Kurunmi's attempt at upholding tradition could, at times, appear tarnished by his almost blind rage and excessive responses. These actions are signs of Kurunmi's personal shortcomings and in no way detract from his concern for his people or the benefits of tradition.

Since Kurunmi is the play's central figure, an analysis of his character is unavoidable. Like Oedipus, Kurunmi has a tendency to over-react in situations that demand greater tact and less vehemence. One such example is Kurunmi's decision to go to war with the new Alafin. He chooses war without consulting his people. It is true that he was king and certainly had the power and authority to declare war. However, as his best warriors later reminded him, consultation would have upheld a second tradition, that of seeking the advice of the War Council.

This tendency towards emotional excessiveness seems to be due to the fact that, in essence, Kurunmi is a loner. In a society where communal identification is of great importance, Kurunmi remains an individual. In his case it is more than just the isolation of command. Perhaps it is this characteristic which has made him such a great general. It is also his greatest burden. Kurunmi leads the group but he is not truly part of it. This explains his tendency to abuse his power and, unintentionally, his followers.

The tragic downfall of Kurunmi can be as easily plotted as his defeat at the hands of his enemies. Though the one may not be dependent on the other, they both follow the same downward spiral. The Ibadan offer greater resistance than Kurunmi had expected and for a time the war seems at a standstill. This same type of stagnation occurs for Kurunmi on a personal level. The following lines eloquently express Kurunmi's misgivings.

    A paddle here, a paddle there,
    yet
    the canoe stands still.
    Is it that I am old?
    A man with fire on his hands moves on.
    Ogun,
    a man with fire on his hands must move on.
    Children of Ibadan have put fire on my head.
    Yet
    I paddle here, I paddle there,
    my canoe stands still and the fire consumes me.

    I want to move,
    Ogun, I want to move.
    This will be my last chance.
    Let me move.
    I am not too old.
    Ogun,
    Sango,
    gods of our fathers,
    this is my last chance in this fight. [11]

Here again, like Oedipus, Kurunmi seems to be manipulated by forces greater than himself. At this point he begins to realize that he may no longer be an asset to his people. Ijaiye is losing the war, and in desperation

Kurunmi makes another tragic error. He loses his last
chance at victory by allowing his forces to cross the Ose
river.

Kurunmi's dying speech reveals not only a defeated
individual but a king and general who has failed his
people.

> When a leader of men has led his people to
> disaster,
> and what remains of his present life
> is but a shadow of his proud past,
> then
> it is time to be leader no more. [12]

Kurunmi has lost the war and his life. Yet, in a sense,
he has still gained a victory. Though he questions his
decision to go to war, he realizes, even at the point of
death, that he was destined to fail. His dying words
illustrate that he could have made no other choices.

> A cow gave birth to a fire.
> She wanted to lick it
> but
> it burned her.
> She wanted to leave it
> but
> she could not
> because it was her own. . .
> her own child,
> her own. . .
> child. [13]

THE TECHNICAL VIEW

Rotimi uses several techniques to emphasize his
thematic concerns. In KURUNMI we see a series of ritual

activities that underscore important events. As was pointed out in the chapter on Soyinka, it is ritual which helps to bridge the gap that exists between man and the gods. It provides the communion that is so essential to man's spiritual existence.

In scene three of act one Kurunmi is shown two bowls by the Alafin's envoy. One contains gunpowder and bullets, the other, the sacred twins of the Ogboni Cult.[14] Kurunmi is to chose one of them. His choice will represent war or peace. This particular ritual is of importance not only because of its sacred nature, but also because of the consequences of Kurunmi's choice.

One of the most dramatic rituals in the play is performed by an Ifa priest and diviner in the Ibadan camp.[15] Even though they are winning the war the Ibadans are still fearful of Kurunmi's power as a warrior. Their fears are increased when they hear that the Egba are joining him. In light of this development, Ibikunle, the Ibadan War General, calls upon Kujenyo, for advice. The old priest performs a ritual of divination with the use of beads. He recites an odu concerning a woman, a gorilla and a river which Ibikunle does not understand. [16] The proper interpretation reveals that the Ibadan will be assured of victory if Kurunmi can be induced to cross the River Ose. Ibikunle is certain that Kurunmi would not be so foolish, and he questions the accuracy of the Ifa Oracle. Kujenyo informs the general that the prophecy is accurate and that Kurunmi can be made to cross the river. At this point the priest suggests an inducement ritual.

> We shall cast a spell on them, my lord. The heads of twenty-one slaves. Entrails of three lizards. Five goats. Seven dogs. Eleven tortoises. Five pigeons. And by daybreak, if the armies of Egba and Ijaiye do not ready themselves to cross the River Ose, chop off my

head, and chop off the head of everyone in my
family born and yet to be born. [17]

The performance of this ritual is not seen in the play.
However, the fact that Kurunmi chooses an unsound battle
plan, suggests the intervention of some supernatural
power.

Rotimi appears to use dance and music as simple
accompaniment for the play's action. A closer look,
however, reveals that the songs present a poetic
statement of the group psyche. Like the choruses of Greek
drama, they relay the group's hopes and aspirations as
well as provide a clear presentation of traditional
values. The chants of praise for Kurunmi and the war
songs of the Egba and Ijaiye seem to blend the
metaphysical with the tangible.

In the chapter on Soyinka we saw how it was possible
to apply the English language to a Yoruba structure with
powerful results. Rotimi handles this technique, which is
more than just a mixture of linguistic elements, quite
well. It is a more sophisticated version of what Dapo
Adelugba has labeled "Yorubanglish." He defines it as:

...a language which is not just Yoruba English
or Yoruba mixed with English but the many-sided
attempt to catch the flavor, tones, rhythms,
emotional and intellectual content of Yoruba
language and thought in an adventurous brand of
English. [18]

An example of Rotimi's technique is the highly
effective manner in which he has Kurunmi express his
tragic descent into despair and defeat. It's uniqueness
lies in the contrast of the softly subdued imagery of his
speech with his earlier brashness. Upon learning of the
deaths of his five sons in scene three, act four,

Kurunmi, for the first time, shows real signs of failure.
He tells several of his warriors that "it is not the
beating of rain-drops that hurts...it is the...the touch
of dew...the soft touch of dew..." [19] Even more eloquent
are the burial instructions given by Kurunmi as he dies.

In the River Ose,
where my honor was buried,
there will you also bury my body.
You will dam the river,
and deep in the sands of its bed,
you will hide my body.
Then you will let the river flow again
for ever,
over the oneness of my body and my honor. [20]

A weakness in KURUNMI is Rotimi's use and treatment
of the white missionaries. The characters are extremely
one dimensional, and they exert no influence on the
play's action. The obvious service provided by their
presence is that they chronicle the events of the war. A
more subtle reason for their inclusion may have been to
underscore the differences between the people of Oyo and
those of Ijaiye. In their relationship with the
missionaries the people of Oyo seem more willing to
compromise on issues of traditional conduct. To Kurunmi
and the people of Ijaiye the missionaries are an annoying
inconvenience.

OVONRAMWEN NOGBAISI

Like KURUNMI, OVONRAMWEN NOGBAISI is also based on
historical events. First produced in 1971, the play was
not published until 1974. Later productions caused a good
deal of controversy in Nigeria. NOGBAISI relates the

events surrounding an 1897 punitive expedition by the
British against the Benin Empire.

PLOT OVERVIEW

A clear understanding of the events in OVONRAMWEN
NOGBAISI also requires a bit of background information
before undertaking the play itself. An important factor
to remember was that by the mid 1800s the British
Protectorate had established its authority over all
Nigerian trade centers except the old and very rich
kingdom of Benin. The then king of Benin, Oba Adolo, had
decreed that his people should not trade with Europeans.
In addition, the British were uneasy about the prominent
role of human sacrifice in the religion of the Bini. The
Bini believed deeply that the gods had to be constantly
propitiated through human sacrifice or disaster would
befall the kingdom. In 1892, five years before the events
of Rotimi's play, Ovonramwen, son of Adolo and new Oba of
Benin, signed a treaty by which Benin was placed under
British protection and human sacrifice was to be
abolished. The treaty also opened trade with the British.
It seems, however, that the provisions of the treaty were
not being implemented with sufficient speed to satisfy
the British. In 1897 Acting Consul General Phillips
decided to visit Ovonramwen in order to press for
quicker compliance with the treaty.[21] At this point in
history the play begins. The play starts with a short
prologue which pictures a group of chained African
prisoners being whipped and forced to march by prison
warders. The prisoner's chant reveals that their
suffering is the worst anyone has ever known. Following a
quick blackout act one opens in the palace of Ovonramwen
where we see the prisoners from the prologue being herded
in. Ovonramwen enters and we learn that the prisoners are
guilty of civil rebellion aimed at disrupting

Ovonramwen's ascension to his father's throne. The prisoners are found guilty and sentenced to death as Ovonramwen asserts his right to rule.

Act one further reveals the strong desire for trade on the part of the British and the equally strong suspicions held by Ovonramwen and his people. An Ifa priest has given a warning to Ovonramwen of a fire and an ocean of blood in which bodies are floating. Believing that the oracle is foretelling the empire's destruction at the hands of the British, Ovonramwen orders the people of his kingdom to "keep watch on the movements of white men, and report at once the route and manner of any strange advance". [22]

In order to quell civil unrest, Ovonramwen chooses one of his most loyal young generals, Ologbosere, to deal with the problem. To prove that he has faith in the young man, Ovonramwen offers the hand of his daughter in marriage which the young man quickly accepts.

With the beginning of act two we hear of the approach of a large number of white men enroute to Benin. This expedition is particularly upsetting due to the approach of the sacred ceremony of Ague, a seven-day ritual in which there can be no visits to Benin or to the Oba by strangers. To break this sacred tradition would bring an eternal curse. The Benin Police are sent to warn the visitors, Phillips and his men, that they must halt their approach and wait two months before they can see the Oba. Phillips agrees to wait for two months, and the police leave with a final warning. It soon becomes clear that Phillips never intended to wait. He continues the expedition almost immediately.

Having learned that Phillips intends to violate their ceremony, Ovonramwen must decide between the sacredness of tradition or the defiance of a powerful enemy. He warns his people to be cautious and retires to deliberate in private. Thinking that the Oba is testing them, Ologbosere and some of the other warriors, take matters into their own hands. Without the knowledge or consent of Ovonramwen, they attack and decapitate Phillips' party. The war which follows the death of Phillips results in the defeat of Benin. The city is destroyed and all of its art work sent to England.

In act three we are shown the trails of the chiefs and the eventual capture and banishment of Ovonramwen. The play closes with an epilogue that pictures the prisoners of the prologue as they chant of the Oba's failing health and the hopelessness of his situation.

THEMATIC CONTENT

One of Rotimi's major concerns in writing OVONRAMWEN NOGBAISI was the economic motivation of the British. Rotimi states:

What I am trying to say in this play is that colonialism, which we now may think is on the decline, is very much in existence, even in independent African nations. Colonialism is in operation in one form or another. The British marched on Benin for purely economic reasons. It goes without saying that even today continued European economic exploitation in Africa, sometimes in very subtle forms, is evident. I think it is up to us, recalling the agonizing experiences of our forebears--like the great god-king Oba Ovonramwen--it is up to us to do all we can to ensure that we compensate for these bitter experiences by making our nation one to be reckoned with. We must try to safeguard our interests, as did our forebears in spite of limited resources and extremely trying conditions. [23]

It was also Rotimi's intent to clarify certain misconceptions concerning Ovonramwen's rule and character. In a background note published in the 1974 edition, Rotimi wrote that Ovonramwen was "a man long portrayed by the biases of Colonial History in the mien of the most abominable sadist, but in actuality, a man more sinned against than he ever sinned." [24]

Rotimi's contention concerning the economic motivation of the British seems to be borne out by historical accounts of the period. [25] However, there are still some doubts concerning the character of Ovonramwen.

In the first act we meet a strong domineering king whose words make clear his intent to rule no matter what the opposition.

> Let the land know this: Ovonramwen Nogbaisi is
> henceforth set to rule as king after the manner
> of his fathers before him. Some men there are
> who think that, by honour of years, or the
> power of position, or by too much love for
> trouble, they can dull the fullness of my glow
> and bring darkness on the empire. But they
> forget... They forget that no matter how long
> and stout the human neck, on top of it must
> always sit a head. Henceforth, a full moon's,
> my glow-dominant, and unopened to rivalry
> throughout the empire. [26]

Rotimi seems well on his way to presenting Ovonramwen as an extremely capable ruler. There is a king-jester relationship much like the one found in Shakespeare's KING LEAR. Through this relationship we see Ovonramwen's wisdom and sense of humor. Also included are a number of short episodic scenes in which we observe Ovonramwen

enthusiastically conducting affairs of state. This show
of kingliness remains intact until Ovonramwen learns that
the white men have disregarded the warning given them
concerning the ceremony of Ague. The Oba's decision at
this point is the most important that he has ever had to
make. Yet, Ovonramwen appears unable to deal with the
situation. He speaks several platitudes comparing the
empire and its ability to handle the intrusion to a
fierce sleeping snake or a cunning cat. However, he makes
no definite decision. He warns his people to be cautious
and exits with the lines: "The eyes...the nose...are one.
Whenever one is hurt the other sheds water. Pray may
nothing hurt the land or the throne." [27] Ovonramwen's
chiefs are left to deliberate on their own. They can only
guess at what their king is thinking. Here again we
notice a Shakespearean flavor as the chiefs misinterpret
the Oba's words much as Sir Pierce of Exton does in
RICHARD II. The resulting decapitations of the white men
horrify Ovonramwen just as the death of Richard does
Bolingbroke.

The play makes no mention of the human sacrifices
which tarnished the character of Ovonramwen in the eyes
of the British. Taken in its proper perspective, the need
for the sacrifices is understandable. What Rotimi does
show us is a human king. He is a determined individual
capable of the same indecision that is common to us all.
Though the consequences of a king's indecision may be
more grave, his moment of weakness does not make him less
a king, just a more believable one. The idea of greed on
the part of the British and the traditional honor of
Ovonramwen seems to have been very popular with Nigerian
audiences. NOGBAISI's production at the Fourth Ife
Festival in 1971 caused the following reaction.

The play's first production was acutely
controversial. Its latter part, after the sack

of Benin, portrays the British so harshly that
some critics felt unsophisticated audiences
might attack the actors playing the officers,
so strong was   the antagonism of the audience
at Ori-Olokun to the whites in the cast. [28]

These highly emotional reactions were matched by the
fervent anticipation of the play's second production.

The famous ancient city of Benin, after whose
historical circumstances the play is set, has
been reported to be gripped with excitement,
since the news of the coming home of OVONRAMWEN
NOGBAISI spread there. There is a rush for
tickets; and the military Governor of the
State, Col. Osaigbovo Ogbemudia, is said to be
delightfully awaiting the arrival of OVONRAMWEN
NOGBAISI. [29]

The passages quoted above are not needed to
substantiate the contemporary relevance of the play.
Mankind will always recognize its fragility, success and
failure, and the uncertainty which can be found in
loyalty and leadership.

THE TECHNICAL VIEW

The creation of an historical drama might appear
fairly simple. The playwright is provided with a
ready-made cast of characters and a chronological series
of events and actions. However, simply to relay or
re-narrate historical data would, in most instances, make
for very dull theatre. It is imperative that the
playwright be able to adapt the historical data to the
limitations of the stage. Creating an historical drama
that is worth theatrical production demands that events

and characters be interpreted and actions intensified in order to support thematic ideas and concerns. The playwright must not be overly concerned with historical fact or chronology. Though he must be, at times, both historian and detective, and in the final analysis he must be more than both. Only then can he present an amplified form of history which is relevant to contemporary concerns and is artisticly pleasing.

For the most part, Rotimi succeeds in his treatment of OVONRAMWEN NOGBAISI. There are, however, certain weaknesses that have resulted from his method of execution.

In act two, after Ovonramwen learns of the decapitations, there is a lull in the play's intensity which gives the impression that we are seeing the start of a second plot. It is at this point that Rotimi is attempting to present what he considers a truer interpretation of certain events. Very little is known about the real motives of the British or the importance that the Bini placed on the empire's cultural integrity. The second half of the play is devoted to the trial of Ovonramwen and his chiefs. It is during this second half of the play that Rotimi attempts his most detailed clarification. He uses a question/answer method to deliver the trial scenes. The method is a legitimate one, but it is a bit overdone. Instead of enhancing it diminishes the play's impact. The characters, which until now had been free and interesting, suddenly become stilted. There is, understandably, less dramatic action in the trial scenes as compared to the first part of the play. We see quite clearly that the British are determined to humiliate Ovonramwen. We also see that the Oba is equally determined to retain his dignity. Both these factors could have been presented much more dramatically and in much less space. The dragging action of the trial scenes lessen the impact of Ovonramwen's escape and eventual recapture. Luckily, this section of the script can be easily altered with no loss of artistic quality or integrity.

A technique which is becoming more prevalent in African theatre is the playwright's intentional mixing of the actors and audience. Such is the case with Rotimi in the trial scenes of NOGBAISI. His stage directions in scene one of act three suggest that:

> ...some chiefs and commonalty move into the auditorium and share seats with members of the audience or simply crouch wherever possible in the aisles, so that the audience now becomes a living part of the action in this scene. [30]

This attempt at making the audience part of the production is seen as an advantage by some African playwrights and critics. They claim that it affords the audience a "vital commentative role" which results in "instant review and criticism of the play as it is performed." [31] The very idea of such activity would be enough to frighten many western producers. In light of Africa's more recent communal past, the great appeal of such there is easy to understand. It is a bit more difficult to prove that this audience involvement does much more that indicate what is superficially pleasing. I question Samuel Asein's description of the "instant acclamation of those sections of the play which show evidence of dramatic excellence, and an equally instantaneous rejection of mediocrity." [32] I doubt that all audiences would react that way.

Rotimi's staging ideas for NOGBAISI and KURUNMI are a further attempt on his part at establishing an identity for African drama. According to Rotimi:

...proscenium in Africa is a dispensable bequest of western imperial culture which, unfortunately, Africans still hold on to with voracious zeal. In traditional presentation where communal involvement is part of the entertainment spirit, spectators sit round the performers. Sometimes the audience forms a three-quarters circle, while the musical ensemble occupies the fourth quarter. All things considered, the arena setting is the only formation that approximates aboriginal theatre arrangement, at least in Africa south of the Sahara." [33]

Rotimi's energetic efforts at establishing a dramatic identity, coupled with his respect for the best of traditional values, promises to add a good deal of vitality to the development of Yoruba theatre.

NOTES

CHAPTER THREE

1
M. Folarin, "Ola Rotimi Interviewed," NEW THEATRE
MAGAZINE, no.2, 1972, p. 5.

2
Ibid., p. 5.

3
Bernth Lindfors, "Interview with Ola Rotimi,"
DEM-SAY: INTERVIEWS WITH EIGHT NIGERIAN WRITERS, Austin:
African and Afro-American Studies and Research Center,
University of Texas, 1974, p. 66.

4
Folarin, p. 7.

5
Ibid., p. 6.

6
Lindfors, p. 68.

7
Atiborpko S.A. Uyovbukerhi, "The Idea of Tragic
Form in NIgerian written in English," Diss., Univ. of
Wisconsin-Madison, 1976, p. 172.

8
Lindfors, p. 67.

9
For an excellent account of the war see Michael
Crowder, A SHORT HISTORY OF NIGERIA (New York: Frederick
A. Praeger, 1962).

10
Ola Rotimi, KURUNMI (Ibadan: University Press
Limited, 1971), pp. 15-16.

11
Ibid., pp. 87-88.

12
Ibid., p. 93.

13
    Ibid., p. 94.

14
    Michael Crowder, A SHORT HISTORY OF NIGERIA (New
York: Frederick A. Praeger, 1962), p. 98.

15
    Ifa is a form of divination connected with the
Yoruba oracle-divinity, Orunmila. It is very popular in
Yorubaland.

16
    Divination beads, called "Opele," are used by Ifa
priest as an instrument for divining. The odu prophetic
sayings are intended to be guidelines for conduct.

17
    Rotimi, p. 73.

18
    Oyin Ogunba, ed., THEATRE IN AFRICA (Ibadan:
Ibadan University Press, 1978), p. 16.

19
    Rotimi, p. 90.

20
    Ibid., p. 93.

21
    For information on the reign of Ovonramwen see
Crowder, A SHORT HISTORY OF NIGERIA, note 14 above.

22
    Ola Rotimi, OVONRAMWEN NOGBAISI (Ibadan:
University press limited, 1974), p. 20.

23
    Lindfors, p. 66.

24
    Rotimi, OVONRAMWEN, p. xi.

25
    An informative account of British involvement with
Benin can be found in Peter Lloyd's PEOPLE OF AFRICA (New
York: Holt, Rinehart and Winston, Inc., 1965).

26
Rotimi, OVONRAMWEN, P. 6.

27
Ibid., p. 35.

28
Robert Wren, "Ola Rotimi: A   Major New talent,"
AFRICA REPORT, no.5, 1961, pp. 29-31.

29
Folarin, p. 5.

30
Rotimi, OVONRAMWEN, p. 51.

31
Samuel Asein, "The Tragic Grandeur   of Ovonramwen
Nogbaisi," NIGERIA MAGAZINE, nos. 110-12, 1974, p. 48.

32
Asein, p. 48.

33
Lindfors, p. 60.

IV

THE FEAR OF AN IMPERFECT FUTURE

THE PLAYWRIGHTS AND THE DRAMAS

The playwrights included in this chapter, Kole Omotoso, Femi Euba, and Bode Sowande, are younger contemporaries of Soyinka and Rotimi. In some instances they are known less for playwriting than for other endeavors which have brought them a good deal of prominence. This in no way diminishes the quality or promise of their plays.

The plays covered in this chapter were culled from a large number of works that were short and more appropriate for other media. Radio drama has always been very popular in Nigeria. The popularity of stage drama has risen, but radio still holds an enviable position due to its ability to quickly reach a large audience and the relative ease of production. There remains a tendency among younger playwrights in Nigeria to write plays that are intended for radio or television.

In addition to age, the playwrights in this chapter also share a common concern for the condition of their countrymen and the side-effects that modernization and progress have had on them. The plays chosen for this chapter paint a true and sometimes harsh picture of Nigeria with an extremely pessimistic regard for the future. Unlike some of the plays by Soyinka and Rotimi, the plays of these young men offer very few answers.

KOLE OMOTOSO

The first play included in this chapter is SHADOWS IN THE HORIZON by Kole Omotoso. Mr. Omotoso is one of Nigeria's foremost novelists. Though he is younger than Achebe or Ekwensi, Omotoso has proven himself with five published novels, three plays, and a collection of short stories.[1] Born in 1943 in Akure, Omotoso was educated at the Universities of Ibadan and Edinburgh.

Stating that he has been influenced more by Soyinka than any other artist, Omotoso is a serious writer with extremely strong commitments. His seriousness and concern for the future of his people is reflected in the following statement.

> I don't think there is any art for art's sake. I don't think it's possible. There has to be a commitment. Even if you write only to entertain, that's a commitment. Art for art's sake is intellectual crap; if you write only for other artists, you're like a snake devouring itself by the tail--a closed circle and nothing more. Whereas if you are committed to communicating with everyone who reads your works, that's a very basic and responsible kind of commitment.
>
> Furthermore, because of the fluid nature of African society, the conscious artist can contribute towards building a new mode of life. Anything he does--the way he presents his characters, the way he lives his own life--is likely to influence what other people are going to do. If he decides to buy a Mercedes Benz and drive it to his village where people don't see five cars collectively a year, then it doesn't

seem to me that he is encouraging anything. But if he is ready to involve himself in the day-to-day way of life of the people and make reasonable suggestions for them so they can improve their lot, then I think he can make quite a big contribution.[2]

FEMI EUBA

Femi Euba's reputation as an actor is unsurpassed among his Nigerian contemporaries. He is especially well known and sought after by producers in England and Nigeria because of his work with the plays of Wole Soyinka. His 1966 portrayal of Lalunkle, from THE LION AND THE JEWEL, was an early indication of his sensitivity as an actor. Euba's 1977 portrayal of Soyinka's Colonel Moses from OPERA WONYOSI, showed that he had not lost that sensitivity.[3] It is a sensitivity which transfers well to his plays.

Educated in Nigeria and a London drama school, Euba has published two radio dramas entitled THE GAME, in 1968 and ABIKU in 1972. Both plays have been produced by the BBC. A RIDDLE OF THE PALMS and CROCODILES are two plays by Euba which were bound as part of a collection at the New York public libarary, but not yet published. This study includes Euba's latest play, THE GULF, written around 1980.

BODE SOWANDE

Of the playwrights recommended for this study by Wole Soyinka, Bode Sowande appears to be the most promising. Having received a French degree from the University of Ife in 1971, Sowande is the youngest of the playwrights included in this study. Like Omotoso, Sowande could also be considered a novelist. OUR MAN THE PRESIDENT, a major novel, was published by Sowande in 1981. It, like his plays, reflects his concern with corruption.

Bode Sowande is also the founder of the Odu Themes drama group in Ibadan. It is one of the few established ensembles in Nigeria. His published plays include A SANCTUS FOR WOMEN, which was first produced in 1976 and is based on a story from Yoruba folklore and mythology. Also included in this study is a sequence of two plays which were first published in 1972 and 1978 respectively. They are THE NIGHT BEFORE and FAREWELL TO BABYLON.

SHADOWS IN THE HORIZON

Published in 1977, SHADOWS IN THE HORIZON bears a strong technical resemblence to the theatre of Rotimi, with regards to audience involvement. It is ideologically close to the strong socio-political concerns that we see in Soyinka. Omotoso describes it as "A play about the combustibility of private property."

PLOT OVERVIEW

The play opens in a public rest area along a major highway. Throughout the play there is the sound of passing motor vehicles.

The first character that we meet is Bamigbade, a politician/businessman, who is carrying an arm full of cars, houses and trunks. Dressed in jewels and white lace, he refers to the items lovingly as his "property." Before long we are introduced to Atewolara, a military/security man and Orimoogunje, an intellectual who is "Professor of Hi-Rated Studies." They too have brought their "property." It is further revealed in act one that the three property owners were classmates in high school. They are very careful to keep their possessions separate and are obviously jealous of each other.

From their conversation we learn that there has been some type of worker revolt which has caused the three of them to flee their homes. The revolt has also caused a spilt in the ranks of the workers who are presently trying to overcome their differences. The trio of property owners know that they must take some type of action before the workers reunite. They decide to compose a petition to their former servants emphasizing the desirability of returning to the status-quo. As act one ends, Bamigbade and Atewolara exit with the petition, leaving the professor, armed with a pistol, to guard all of the property.

As act two begins Orimoogunje is still alone with the property and is becoming more and more envious of the possessions of his colleagues. After a bit of soul searching the professor decides to kill his fellow property owners when they return and take all of the property for himself. At this point a procession of Aladura enter singing praises. The professor joins the enthusiastic congregation in their praises and prayers. The prayers are not for peace or salvation but for power and riches.

As the Aladura leave Orimoogunje is joined by Bibilari and Alogbo, leaders of the workers' union. They tell the professor of their suffering and how their revolt will change their deplorable conditions. They easily disarm Orimoogunje and inform him that the union has been searching for him and the other property owners. They further inform him of their intention to confiscate the property that he has been guarding in the name of their union. As the two union leaders conduct an inventory of the property, Atewolara and Bamigbade return. They quickly retrieve the gun from the workers and accuse them, along with the professor, of plotting to steal their property. The two workers suddenly flee leaving Orimoogunje to be slowly strangled by Atewolara as act two ends.

In act three the workers are finally united and seem to have the upper hand. There is a massive rally at which Alogbo and Bibilari are holding a public inquiry into the activities of Bamigbade and Atewolara. In accordance with their findings Bamigbade is sentenced to death. To the astonishment of Bamigbade, his partner in theft and murder is not condemned. It seems that the security man has been "performing his duty" all along. As the act ends Bamigbade is shot. Atewolara immediately claims all property as his own and informs all present that the workers' union is to be disbanded.

Atewolara instals himself as king with the support of the military. As act four begins, he is in the process of granting audience to various groups which have come to pay him homage. The only persons not present are the former leaders of the Workers Union. When they finally arrive they insult the new dictator and demand that he negotiate with them. Atewolara agrees to negotiate while secretly ordering the death of Bibilari and Alogbo. Unfortunately for Atewolara these deaths so outrage and disgust his followers that they join the union against him. To Atewolara's horror, the two groups burn his throne as the play ends.

THEMATIC CONTENT

Omotoso's major thematic concern in SHADOWS is quite clear. The overwhelming avarice displayed by the three main characters indicates that the playwright regards the excessive greed as the foundation for many other evils. Omotoso reveals that this infectious greediness is strong in the area of politics, business, the military, and even among the intellectuals. We have seen some of these same groups condemned before. However, Omotoso leaves no segment of society untouched. In act two we see the Aladura leader demanding money for aiding the professor in his prayers for power and riches. It seems that the church, in the eyes of Omotoso, is just as corrupt as the community it serves. There is also little hope that any salvation is to be found in the more traditional segments of society. There is ample proof of this after Atewolara declares himself king. The first group to present itself to the new dictator is a group of traditional rulers who realize that Atewolara will do nothing for the betterment of his people. Despite their awareness, the rulers make no protest. They speak only of shallow ideas that will lead to peaceful co-existence with the new leader. Audience is also given to a group of market women who are extremely important to the survival of traditional society. The women make it immediately clear that they have come to love the "profit motive" more than motherhood. They assure Atewolara that he has their complete support and understanding.

Not even the workers' union, which is supposed to represent the masses, can claim complete freedom from corruption or offer a real solution. They see their salvation in the same tyrannical vision that oppresses them. Before Bamigbade is executed by the union members in act three, they inform him that they have been working with Atewolara in his capacity as an undercover agent. Perhaps they believe that the tyranny of one man will be less harsh than the tyranny of a system. Especially if the tyrant is indebted to them. There is a hint of this in the dialogue spoken during Bamigbade's trial.

BAMIGBADE: You want to impose a tyranny of the union on the country?

ALOGBO: The tyranny already exists. We want

to use it to the advantage of all. If tyranny
must exist, let it dedicate itself to the
eradication of...
ATEWOLARA: Freedom of speech?
ALOGBO: In hunger, anger, or about what?
ATEWOLARA: Freedom of movement?
ALOGBO: In search of shelter or simply
wondering about shelter?
ATEWOLARA: Freedom of assembly?
ALOGBO: In state hospitals or in private
bucheries?
BIBILARI: Only the tyranny that frees
ALOGBO: man from hunger. From the vagueries of
tomorrow. And the salt-watertrap.
         The tyranny of a time!
ATEWOLARA: We are in for a strangle hold on
thought. Going under growing restrictions. And
forced into compulsory conformity.
ALOGBO: We merely mortgage today for a tomorrow
of fulfilment.[4]

To their dismay Atewolara outlaws their union. They
now find themselves in a worse predicament than before
their collaboration.

The end of act four offers, symbolically, what might
be the only answer to the dilemma. By having the union
members and Atewolara's men join in burning the throne,
Omotoso seems to advocate a fresh beginning free of any
existing system. As the throne burns, the property of
Atewolara is also thrown on the fire. There is no talk of
property consfication as was heard in act two. To
emphasize the desire for a new beginning Omotoso directs
that the entire set be put to the torch. Through the
flames we hear Atewolara make the following plea: "No,
you cannot build from ashes," as the play ends.

THE TECHNICAL VIEW

An important concern for any western producer would be the fact that there are no translations provided for the Yoruba passages which are used in SHADOWS IN THE HORIZON. Of particular concern would be the songs of praise and prayers during the Aladura scene. There are also several passages in acts three and four which might prove insurmountable. Translations of all passages and phrases are provided in a later appendix.

Omotoso's production technique is similar to those of Rotimi and Soyinka. Like Rotimi, he tries to break the traditional barriers that separate audience and actor. This is most obvious during the trial scene when the workers seat themselves in various sections of the audience. There is not as great an attempt at direct audience involvement as we have seen in Rotimi; however, there are points at which actors speak directly to the audience. An example is the old woman who approaches audience members concerning the translation of her son's letter.

Omotoso admits that he is concerned with entertainment. His concern may be no greater than that of the other playwrights discussed here, but he is the first to admit it freely and with considerable emphasis.

In Yoruba society we are interested in entertainment as well as instruction. Possibly, entertainment comes first. People have to be entertained, but maybe afterwards they'll want to reflect on what they have been entertained with. They can draw messages from it. They are interested in both the comic and the serious dimensions of a story.[5]

Omotoso's use of English is reminiscent of the sophistication that we saw in Soyinka's use of the language. The cleverness of Omotoso's dialogue is best seen in the speech of submission given by the traditional rulers in act four. Omotoso has the speaker insult Atewolara while appearing to praise him. To adequately demonstrate this cleverness the passage should be quoted in its entirety.

> Once more
> It is our chore
> To welcome--Or
> Shall we say
> To ensure our way
> In the new day.
> Creepers need trees
> Leaves need breeze
> To wave as they please.
> We are the people's trunks
> Their plunks
> Or else they are skunks.
> Some people have suggested
> That emirs,obas and obis be arrested
> Since their good is not attested.
> But tell me
> Who else are the people's epitome?
> His excellency is not to answer me.
> Your singular deed
> Meets the peoples' need
> At this hour of great greed.
> Your excellency
> Is not unconnected with royalty
> And the dictates of pageantry.
> So
> Whatever we with you grow
> Such will our people sow.

Once, Your excellency, more
It is my, Your excellency, chore
To, Your excellency, welcome. Or
Shall I pray
That our Gods ensure your way
As your star lights a new day.
Finally,
And I needn't unneccessarily
Take the time of Your excellency,
But let me assure you
What you want we will do
And we all the consequences will rue.[6]

Unlike Rotimi, Omotoso does not appear to be making any concerted effort at developing a new or unique approach in his use of the English language. He explains his approach this way.

I have attempted quite a lot of things, but I think, because of my education, I write better in English than in Yoruba. I have been involved in western things for too long, and I've read more in English than I've read in Yoruba. At one time I wanted to write in Yoruba, and from time to time I still wonder if I should be writing in Yoruba or in English. It was only recently that I decided it didn't really matter much which choice I made.[7]

In evaluating the work of Kole Omotoso the characteristics most prominent and pleasing are his clever usage of thought and language, his frugality of plot, and his commitment to truth.

THE GULF

Labled an "extended metaphor" by its playwright, THE
GULF deals with western mechanization and its effect on
African culture. Though there is nothing unique about
such a treatise, Euba adds an interesting twist. THE GULF
is the only play in this study in which we see a Nigerian
playwright attempting to address the cultural
conditioning of Afro-Americans as well as his own people.

PLOT OVERVIEW

The play opens with a rather long prologue involving
Yangi, a bus driver, and a number of imaginary
passengers. Through these imaginary interactions Yangi
demonstrates the philosophy of the road and the rather
amoral attitude of drivers. It is the same chaotic
situation that we saw in Soyinka's play, THE ROAD. The
prologue ends with the crash of Yangi's bus in which
almost all of his passengers are killed.

In part one several familiar character types are
introduced. We meet Dabiri, a nervous, corrupt policeman,
a young intellectual reporter referred to by the others
as "Inside-Out," and Gold, an attractive Afro-American
tourist.

Dabiri seems quite intent on finding the driver of
the death bus, the wreckage of which has mysteriously
disappeared. During his conversation with the reporter we
learn that there have been other strange occurences
related to highway accidents.

Dabiri exits as Gold enters seeking directions to an
old slave fort which has been converted into a
combination cultural center/museum. She is described by
Euba as being "enthusiastic and self-assertive." In her
conversation with the reporter we also learn that she is
quite defensive about her background. As she leaves for

the fort, Yangi enters with a slaughtered dog and performs a ritual of appeasement to the god Ogun. While the reporter watches from the shadows, Dabiri enters and we learn that the policeman has agreed to take a bribe from Yangi and his father so that Yangi can avoid the criminal charges which would result from his recent accident. As part one ends Dabiri and Yangi make a date for the delivery of the bribe.

In part one scene two, we meet a very westernized Highway Commissioner who is just returning from a trip to America where he had hoped to find some remedies for the horrible traffic accidents in his country. We further learn that he is having an affair with his secretary who acts more like a wife than a secretary. He is also constantly trying to avoid Babalorisha, a traditional religious leader and the father of Yangi, the bus driver. It seems that the old man wants the Commissioner to employ traditional methods in dealing with the problems of the road instead of the western techniques, which seem to be of little use.

The old man later admits to the Commissioner that he was responsible for the disappearence of the bus wreckage. He claims that he was obeying the orders of Ogun and that the accident was not his son's fault. Babalorisha further invites the Commissioner to attend a ceremony in honor of Ogun. The Commissioner refuses.

Part two scene one is devoted to Gold and the reporter as they discuss the merits of Ogun and traditional beliefs. Dabiri enters near the end of the scene and drunkenly tries to justify his taking of bribes.

The second scene reveals the location of the Ogun ceremony and the presence of the Commissioner in traditional dress. He has been threatened and blackmailed into attending by Babalorisha. The old priest insists that he only wants what is best for the Commissioner and the people. The Commissioner must, according to Babalorisha, return to the ideas of his fathers and renounce his western habits. He further informs the Commissioner that Ogun has demanded the sacrifice of his son Yangi and that he wants the Commissioner to take part. The Commissioner tries to resist but finally succumbs to the threats of Babalorisha.

Yangi's sacrifice is the subject of scene three. Babalorisha performs an elaborate ceremony before he approaches his son with the sacrificial knife. Unable to cope with what he is witnessing, the Commissioner interrupts the proceedings and promises to do all that he can to remedy the highway situation. He further promises that all actions on his part will be dedicated to and carried out in the name of Ogun.

Babalorisha explains that he had never intended to actually kill his son. He explains that the traditionalists are just as confused by progress and modernization as anyone else. He believes that there must be compromise even if it is only a temporary answer. As the scene ends the two men agree to try and work out their differences.

In the fourth and final scene we learn that Gold has been attacked by Yangi at the slave fort. While trying to rape her, he was shot and killed by his victim, who tells the story to the reporter. Inside-Out advises Gold not to tell the police but to seek help from the Commissioner. As the play closes the reporter condemns the country's legal system and lack of true morality.

THEMATIC CONTENT

Euba's chief concern is the manner in which his people cope with the uncertainty of cultural change. Neither the borrowed western techniques nor what Euba refers to as traditional "ritualistic manifestations" seem to help very much. The principal culprit is confusion. It is a condition which permeates every situation and the mind of all of Euba's characters. The confusion is apparently a result of the clash between the state of contentment, which usually accompanies the observance of tradition, and the intriguing lure of modernization, which is often disturbing.

This state of perplexity manifests itself most clearly in Yangi. His situation is well understood by the reporter Inside-Out. He tells Gold:

> ...make a scapegoat of one offender out of the ninety percent of road drivers who, like him, do not know the link between recklessness and death? ...believing that nothing can happen to them, that is, as long as the traditional laws are observed.[8]

Yangi's own words support the reporter's contention. In explaining his ethics, Yangi states;

> ...its only fair that we test our skills on the new road, master this sharp bend and that curve, this cross-roads and that stop sign, this bridge and that hill! We must learn to Accelerate through them all within the shortest of time. Never get caught crawling up that hill like a snail, for you will certainly be over taken! What's the use of a bend or a stop sign, if you cannot show that you are a

> master-manouvrer at it! The rule is there's no
> rule, but be concerned with your self alone,
> for nobody else matters![9]

Even though Inside-Out appears to understand Yangi's
situation, he is himself just as unsure of how to deal
with his own spiritual crisis. When questioned by Gold
concerning the merits of his professed socialism versus
capitalism, Inside-Out voices his own dilemma.

> Okay, where's my supposed revolutionary
> spirit?...I'm not saying it's easy. But at
> times I wonder whether what we really want is
> the change, or the good things we can grab
> from, say, two evils. Its another big joke!
> Like putting together the components of a bad
> accident.[10]

The policeman, Dabiri, seems to be a step beyond the
specific concerns expressed by the reporter. Dabiri is
concerned with justifying his personal corruption. His
greatest justification is his perception that everyone is
corrupt. The only difference that he sees between himself
and everyone else is a matter of method and degree.
Speaking specifically about the reporter, he expresses
his view to the audience at the end of the first scene in
part two.

> ...I won't be surprised at all if he does
> actually do a back-hand business here and
> there. Might not be much...might not even be
> money. But, damn it, a bribe is a
> bribe!...Every Goddamn, living body in this
> city does it! I may say so! I, Dabiri, the
> indefatigable, Ogun-conditioned, Esu-supported,
> bribe-pimpled fool...I say so![11]

Neither of the two remaining characters, the commissioner nor Babalorisha, is free from the paradoxes faced by the others. They seem to be more sure of themselves and their convictions, but they are betrayed by their actions. The commissioner certainly displays all the trappings of western modernization but he is also guilty of a possibly negative side effect. The commissioner admits that in the past, only half of allotted funds have been properly spent. According to the commissioner:

> Oh no, it wasn't a case of misappropriation of funds. At least not intentional. I was trying to save on the economy of the country, but I have since been the wiser for that intent--the money saved went into wrong hands.[12]

As for Babalorisha, we learn through his son Yangi that despite his constant attempts at returning the Commissioner to honest traditional values, the old priest is bribing Dabiri on Yangi's behalf. He even admits to a clever selfishness whenever it serves his purposes.

> Every rule, argument, law doctrine...every tradition, religion, belief or constitution, is capable of being meaning meaningless and meaningful at the same time. It is a matter of opinion...of conviction?...All we need do is follow a path, a single path. The only path most meaning to us.[13]

The logical answer to the dilemma described by Euba is a rational synthesis of traditional observance with that which is most beneficial in western modernization. The problem is the speed with which such a transformation must take place. Any attempt at artificial acceleration of the process can be disastrous. Impatience with the disparity that exists between the promise of progress and the fulfillment of that promise makes it extremely difficult to wait for a natural synthesis. In light of this fact, the volatile situations that we find throughout Africa should not be too surprising. Perhaps the only answer is the trial and error of concerted compromise.

THE TECHNICAL VIEW

As with the latter plays of Soyinka, THE GULF has a short glossary accompanying it which defines fully the Yoruba terms used in the play. There is little reason for worry concerning translation. Euba's use of English is quite adequate and his dialogue straightforward. The reader will not find the sophistication of Soyinka or the cleverness of Omotoso. This may be due, in part, to the fact that Soyinka and Omotoso have a good deal more scholarly training in the language than does Euba.

The fact that Euba is an actor first and a playwright second tends to effect his dramaturgy. An actor of his stature should certainly understand what constitutes a well developed character. When we view his characters individually we find that each of them is indeed well done and would provide a worthwhile challenge to any actor. The problem is a stiffness which exists in the characters' inter-relationships. The obvious and expected interactions, such as the adversarial relationship of Babalorisha and the commissioner, work quite well. It is the more subtle relationships which seem incomplete. The best example is the relationship of Gold to Inside-Out. It is difficult to understand her sudden changes. She is very antagonistic toward the reporter at the outset. We see no indication of romantic involvement or growth in personal respect, yet, later in the play the antagonism seems to have completely disappeared.

It is also difficult to gauge the relationship between Inside-Out and the Commissioner. Are they true friends with certain philosophical differences or do they feign these differences for the benefit of others? The existence of these questions could prove to be a welcome challenge, instead of a distressing problem, to the director who does more than simply follow schematics. They certainly are not serious enough to make the play unworthy of production.

Euba's staging technique is very similar to what we have seen in Rotimi and Omotoso. The play lends itself to a non-proscenium type of production. Euba employs less direct audience involvement than does Rotimi and Omotoso. We find his characters speaking directly to the audience, but there is no physical interaction. The only stage direction which might cause some hesitation is found at the beginning of scene two in the second part. Euba states that the "scene is the same as before, but from a different viewpoint." Not only is it difficult to understand what the playwright means by "another viewpoint," there is also no reason given for needing a different viewpoint. The scene that precedes this one involves Gold, Inside-Out and Dabiri. It takes place on a park bench and is one of the longest scenes in the play. It would be much better to change the entire setting than to simply shift viewpoints. The scene which follows is between the Commissioner and Babalorisha. It reveals the final confrontation of will and ideas between the two and should be staged in a more confined setting.

The warning given in the introduction against the "Yoruba culture trap" should be taken here when considering the play's last scene. In the preceding scene we had been given a feeling of satisfaction and finality by the promise of the Commissioner and Babalorisha to work together in an effort to better serve all of their people. Suddenly, in the following and final scene, we find that Gold has been led through the fort's dark passages by Babalorisha to his son Yangi who attempts to rape her. She kills Yangi with a pistol from her purse and flees. She is advised by Inside-Out not to go to the police but to seek help from the Commissioner.

The question, of course, is why include the scene at all after what appeared to be a perfect ending in the preceding scene. The bewilderment is not due to any incomprehensible factor of Yoruba culture or of Euba's psyche. The reason is obscure because of technique and apparent indecision. If this scene was to be included at all it should have been placed before the one that precedes it. It appears to have been an afterthought on the part of the playwright and simply misplaced. The motivation for the attempted rape is first given in part one scene two. Gold says that Babalorisha called her the daughter of Ogun and said that Ogun had brought her home from America to honor him. Perhaps that honor is a ritual rape. Even if we accept this interpretation it is almost impossible to accept any honest religious involvement on the part of Babalorisha. In the last scene with the Commissioner he proves himself an unscrupulous opportunist. Whatever Euba's intention, the scene would have been much less troublesome with proper placement and careful development.

THE NIGHT BEFORE

AND

FAREWELL TO BABYLON

Of the four plays covered in this chapter, Sowande's THE NIGHT BEFORE best illustrates the fear of an imperfect future alluded to in the chapter subtitle. This fear also exists in the minds of many Africans. Time and time again during the post independence period, this fear has been confirmed in virtually every African nation. There is the fear of dictatorship, the fear of war, starvation, and suffering. There is also the fear addressed by Euba in the preceding play. The fear of a life without direction, without meaning or fulfillment. FAREWELL TO BABYLON tries to address these fears and offer a measure of quiescence if not the contentment of true hopefulness.

FAREWELL TO BABYLON was written and published as a sequel to THE NIGHT BEFORE. Both plays will be analyzed in the same discussion with distinctions being made where necessary.

PLOT OVERVIEW

In THE NIGHT BEFORE we meet six university students on the eve of their graduation. They have gathered in a bamboo drinking shack to celebrate. They are all preoccupied with the same uncertainties and aspirations as all young people who find themselves moving toward an uncharted future. There is, however, a severity in their anticipation that borders on pure dread. This fear of the future is most evident in the character of Onita. He is a young, eccentric sculptor whose pessimism and fear threatens to spoil the celebration. The character best able to cope with the situation is Moniran, the class president and natural leader of the group. The remaining characters fall somewhere between these two. There is Nibidi, the materialist, who constantly talks of the wealth that his education will bring him. There are Dabira and Ibilola, the young lovers who choose to deal with each other rather than the worrisome future. The last character is Moye, the follower. He tries to be everything to everyone. We soon learn that all of the students entered the university thinking that it would solve all of their problems and guarantee their futures. They quickly discovered that they would have to, in the final analysis, make their own decisions. It was quite unsettling to learn that there were no pre-packaged answers to the meaning of life and existence.

While enjoying their palm-wine, they tell of classmates who, because of insanity, suicide, or disillusionment, have failed to reach graduation. It becomes increasingly evident that none of the survivors are really sure who is more fortunate, they or the comrades they've lost along the way.

The central conflict which moves this one scene drama along is a personal animosity and rivalry between Onita and Dabira. A romantic involvement had existed between Onita and Ibilola before the young woman became engaged to Dabira. That involvement is now resurfacing, and the tension between Dabira and Onita begins to build. Added to this is the fact that Dabira has always felt inferior to Onita because of his intellect and the ease with which he performed his academic tasks.

All of the students, to some degree, have allowed themselves to picture their university degrees as passports to a secure future. They cling to these uncertain hopes even after they have seen evidence to the contrary. This false sense of security is challenged once again when the climatic confrontation between Onita and Dabira takes place. While engaged in conversation with Moniran, Dabira fails to notice that Ibilola has left with Onita. When they return Ibilola informs him that she is still in love with Onita despite what she and Dabira have meant to each other. Dabira's violent reaction is checked by Moniran who tries to put what has happened into a rational perspective. Unmoved by Moniran's rationalizing, Dabira neatly folds his graduation gown and places it on the fire. The play ends as the others watch the burning gown and a loudspeaker announces the forthcoming graduation exercises.

THE NIGHT BEFORE works well as a short one act play. It works even better when done in conjunction with FAREWELL TO BABYLON. It serves well as a first act, providing an excellent exposition. The only characters held over from THE NIGHT BEFORE are Onita and Moniran. We learn that Moniran has become chief of a state security organization and that he is referred to as "The Octopus." Onita has been appointed Doctor of Philosophy at the state university.

As the play opens we find Moniran and a fellow security officer, Kaago, preparing a female agent, Jolomi, for the infiltration of a farmers' group. It appears that the country is in the grips of inflation, food shortages and a farmers' revolt. This is in addition to an iron-fisted dictator who has appointed himself Field Marshal and President, "The Supreme Eagle of the Realm." Kaago thinks that a military solution is the only method of dealing with the revolting farmers. Moniran disagrees and orders Kaago to support the planned espionage. At this point Sowande begins to reveal certain interesting facts. After learning of a romantic involvement between Moniran and Jolomi, we see in scene three, that Onita has been arrested and jailed for what were considered treasonous statements in his recently published book. Onita also has a large student following because of his declared opposition to the government. Onita is shocked to learn that his former classmate, Moniran, is The Octopus, the dreaded, faceless chief of security. While undergoing interrogation Onita spits in Moniran's eyes and refuses to cooperate any further. The scene ends with Onita on the cell floor gasping for breath after a brief beating at the hands of Kaago.

Almost immediately we learn that Moniran is plotting the overthrow of the President with the assistance of a military conspirator named Major Kasa. Their intention is to establish a democratic coalition to rule the country. The danger of discovery has forced Moniran to keep his plans a secret even from Jolomi, his lover and the agent whom he has sent on an extremely dangerous mission. We discover that the purpose of Jolomi's mission is the same as the point of Onita's interrogation. Moniran is trying to find Dansaki, head of the farmers' revolt, so that he can inform him of the planned coup d'etat.

Major Kasa informs Moniran that the soldiers directly under his command and the rest of the country seem ready for the overthrow. Moniran, however, is very cautious saying he wants nothing left to chance. While waiting for the perfect moment, Moniran detects a worsening of the situation, and he begins to wonder if he has, perhaps, waited too long. He has lost contact with Jolomi, and he is finding it difficult to protect Onita without revealing his intentions. Moniran decides that the coup should take place while the Field Marshal is out of the country at a meeting of the Organization of African Brotherhood. He is certain of this when he learns, after the Field Marshal's departure, that Onita has been murdered by a fellow prisoner. The murderer, a psychopath named Cookie, was placed in Onita's cell by order of the Field Marshal.

Major Kasa is ordered by Moniran to arrest Kaago and carry out the overthrow without delay. Once the takeover is well under way Moniran leaves to search for Jolomi. He finds her with the farmers who had earlier discovered that Jolomi was a spy for which they branded her on both cheeks. The farmers are assured by Moniran that the country's new leader, Major Kasa, is waiting for them to help form the new government. The play ends with Moniran trying to console Jolomi who informs him that her ordeal at the hands of the farmers has changed her outlook on life, including her affection for him.

THEMATIC CONTENT

Sowande's concern for tyranny and dictators is quite evident in both THE NIGHT BEFORE and FAREWELL TO BABYLON. What he has accomplished is the presentation of two periods in the lives of two of his characters. This concern is addressed, first, by the young and often naive university students, and second, by these same individuals some ten years later. The desire for an alternative society is the thread which runs through both plays and holds them together. It may be impossible totally to appreciate Sowande's hatred of dictators without having lived under a dictatorship. However, it is easier to understand the fear and frustration. In the introductory notes for THE NIGHT BEFORE, Sowande wrote:

While the search for "alternatives" continues among conscious progressives, "accidents" and repressions occur against the struggle, often with methodic planning. It is for this reason that I dedicate this play to the "unknown students" lying in graves, or in lunatic asylums or prison cells of those dictators who litter what they call the "Free World."[14]

FAREWELL TO BABYLON is preceded by a poem entitled "Prayer in a Dictatorship." The last verse of the poem reads:

Pray rise Judas and resurrect in this rank,
perform a duty,
for once,
a wholesome duty;
Be Brutus to their Nero,
Forsake this dictator, his retainers; dislodge

them!
Their conscience poured into fire,
to yield its lava or cast of gold-divine--
Before damnation day-Before D-Day.
And Earth and Heaven will say, Amen for ever.[15]

The students in THE NIGHT BEFORE are as disillusioned by their ineffectualness as they are by what they perceive to be a repressive, malevolent society. Their inability to effect change is made all the more disheartening by the fact that they have been taught that they can make a difference. It appears the prospect of failure has never been addressed. Onita and Moye parody a conversation with the Vice Chancellor of their university. Moye is the Vice Chancellor while Onita plays himself. The parody might give some idea of their university atmosphere and its value.

ONITA: Sir, I am here to learn.
To be exact, sir, to be an intellectual.
MOYE: And an intellectual you will be.
ONITA: So I can solve all the problems of my people.
Cure their indifference to time and their ever willingness to laugh.
MOYE: Emotionalism can be explained.
ONITA: Is that why we are a laughing people?
MOYE: You will find definitions to explain it.
ONITA: And sir, I need a tag against my name. A tag like yours. Mr. Onita; Bachelor in Nation Building; M.A. in the Liberation Studies of Africa. Ph.D. in Humanitarian Politics, etc. etc.etc.
MOYE: You will fulfill your ambitions--we are only masters in nation building. We professors

and doctors are nothing but masters. Our humble
task is to make masters out of you.[16]

Just surviving until graduation has not been, in
itself, a satisfying or uplifting accomplishment. It is
true that many were not strong enough to survive;
however, the survivors seem only to have prolonged their
agony. This graduation eve seems to be no different from
any other night on which the promise of a new day demands
the fortification provided by palm-wine.

There appears to have been little difference between
the atmosphere which existed in African universities
during the sixties and that which existed in other
universities, especially those in America. Sowande's
description of life at his university seems all too
familiar.

The gathering was always in between the running
of the rag-underground press, moods of
rebellion, and downright disillusionment. The
campus vibrated with politics and even
pentecostal evangelism, with some students
easily bridging the two disciplines. Most felt
the dread beyond and within the superficial
protection of the institution.[17]

The fear which plagues the students of THE NIGHT
BEFORE has diminished very little in FAREWELL TO BABYLON.
An excellent example is the character of Onita. In THE
NIGHT BEFORE he compares the past to a "ghost that haunts
me with malice. Is it not enough to dread the future, to
pause, to be ready for the struggles? Must you reach out
from the grave of memories?"[18] Being older and more
experienced he is better able to understand his fear in
FAREWELL TO BABYLON; however, his answer to dealing with
it is simply to disregard it. He tells Moniran that he is

giving up the university and that he wishes to spend the rest of his life as a farmer. He chooses this path, not because he admires the farmers or the worth of farming. He does it simply to escape the chaos of his life.

Moniran, unlike Onita, has a definite plan for dealing with the illness of his society. Luckily, his position affords him the opportunity. He moves with the same ease in FAREWELL TO BABYLON as he did in THE NIGHT BEFORE. Not everyone possesses the natural ability for leadership and diplomacy that we see in Moniran. Sowande may be telling us that the presence of such a person is necessary if there are to be effective attempts at change. Moniran, however, is not the messianic figure that we saw in the early works of Soyinka. He is an efficient functionary whose abilities happen to be operating on the side of the revolutionaries. Though he speaks the same revolutionary words, they lack the passionate conviction of Onita. Moniran's words are calculated and almost scientific in their application. In a speech to the audience near the beginning of FAREWELL TO BABYLON, Moniran states:

> There is more to be said about Babylon and the fire that will destroy it. There is more to be said about everything, but for now, let all ears be glued to the earth. Maybe in the unseen forces that hold a nation together a reason will be found for our predicament. Yours and mine. The only way to foil the siege of the earth, when it rises against you, is to capture its rhythm. The only way to topple a giant is to use the impetus of his onrush, an ancient technique of wrestling.[19]

This mechanical precision is, in part, the reason for Jolomi's decision at the end of the play, to leave

Moniran. When Moniran finally finds her after the coup it is obvious that Jolomi feels she has been sacrificed in the name of the revolution. She waits for Moniran to console her and to, at least, make an attempt at explaining why he used her as he did. Moniran replies that the risks were necessary. He tells her that plastic surgery will remove the scars from her face and that she has been promoted. The play ends with the following dialogue.

> Jolomi: Say it, Moniran. Like a human being.
> Not like a controlled self-powered master-machine. Say it. What do you want from me?
> MONIRAN: Your...affection as always intended.
> JOLOMI: I cannot help you, Moniran. It takes something deeper. Find it your self.
> MONIRAN: [Turns to the audience.]
> You are born alone.
> You dream to exist and live with others.
> Then you die alone and humanity buries you like Dr. Onita
> Only if you are a hero.[20]

There is a school of thought which states that the greatest reward for self-sacrifice must come from the satisfaction of knowing that the sacrificial effort, regardless of its success or failure, was a true and honest one. Whether or not Sowande ever subscribed to such an idea is debatable. However, the character who rids the country of Sowande's dreaded dictator does not appear truly to need or seek such personal compensation. Moniran operates as a well-trained mechanic who has finished one job and is ready to move to the next. Perhaps it is not so unreasonable to imagine a revolution conducted with the same highly technical computerized

efficiency that we now use to market toothpaste or
conduct political campaigns. The most important factor
now appears to be the desired results with little regard
for method. Sowande's Moniran is almost the complete
opposite of Eman or Olunde, the passionate scapegoats of
Soyinka.

It may be that the self-centered attitude of Onita
is the only practical answer. He gives the following
advice to one of his young admirers.

> Spread your blanket, son, in that corner. Sit
> on it in silence. Your excitement will die
> down. If you care to listen, I will tell you
> why no one should take me as a mentor or a
> guru. I am no Socrates, son, look for your
> messiah in yourself! The time of messiahs is
> over. Don't let any hypocrite deceive you.
> There is death in this place but there is life
> in your mind. And that is stronger.[21]

Would our existence be more satisfying if we were
only to concern ourselves with our personal liberation
and leave the rest to the Monirans among us? Such
questions are indeed worth considering, and it is to
Sowande's credit that he is able to pose them.

THE TECHNICAL VIEW

Sowande's stagecraft contains many of the same
elements already discussed in preceding analyses. The
tendency to have the actors, on occasion, speak directly
to the audience is an example. This technique has
completely replaced the more familiar soliloquy often
used to relay the character's internal thought when alone

on stage. It is also used, as might be expected, to inform and to elicit certain reactions from the audience. Near the opening of THE NIGHT BEFORE, Onita turns to the audience and tells them of the hope and thirst for knowledge that the students had upon entering the university. Near the end of the first scene in FAREWELL TO BABYLON, the actors urge the audience to join them in the singing of "We Shall Overcome." There is, however, none of the direct invasion of the audience space that we saw in Omotoso and Rotimi.

The use of pantomime, which we first saw in Soyinka, and to a lesser degree in Rotimi, is also present in FAREWELL TO BABYLON. In the first scene the characters of Yulli and Cookie mime the actions as Onita tells the story of the elephant who became king. It is a parable on the importance of truth.

During the scenes in jail, Onita and the other prisoners often act out the stories that they tell. This helps to heighten the impact of the speaker's words. An excellent example is Sowande's use of the swing rhythm from an African pentecostal church song entitled "Spread Ye the word! Jesus is coming!" The song is delivered in Yoruba while the participants, the prisoners, dance in pentecostal style. Onita then translates the song and declares that the "spreading word" is Communism and Socialism and warns that everyone should "Get on your Marx." The point of this little interlude, according to Onita, is to point up the danger of mindlessly memorizing values. There is always the possibility that the values will become meaningless by their repetition and start to breed dogmas.

To conclude this discussion of Sowande's plays, mention should be made of his somewhat unconventional choice of a group of farmers as the revolutionary element in FAREWELL TO BABYLON. The choice was interesting and appropriate. Of the previous plays in which we have encountered revolutionaries, only Soyinka's KONGI'S HARVEST used the farmer as an element of revolution. Soyinka, however, does little more than mention a farmers' cooperative. Their leader, Daodu, is a city dweller first and a farmer only by association. Most of the revolutionaries in African drama have been city dwellers much like the ones that we see in Omotoso's SHADOWS IN THE HORIZONS. The idea of the oppressed city laborer is in keeping with the majority of revolutionary dramas that have existed in the West.

This switching of revolutionary elements provides, from a technical point of view, a strong emotional context for the play and an even stronger emotional link with the audience. This is particularly true in a country so heavily dependent on agriculture. Note the following dialogue in which the farmers' situation is exposed. The first statement represents a farmer's view.

Oduloju: What do we get in return?
We cannot afford to live well:we don't earn enough. People come and take our photographs, record our songs and call us the real African. Who is the real African? A man who cultivates the land and feeds a nation but starves in his own hut?
Dansaki: We want to live comfortably. It is a hot country. We want fans, air conditioners, refrigerators. We want to ride in cars, because we feed this nation. It is not only the gold mines of the North or the oil of the South. The earth is for man, why do you not want to pay for its lease from nature?[22]

Next is a quote by Yulli which he says he memorized from Onita's book.

It can be no accident that one of the greatest prayers man was taught has this phrase "God give us this day our daily bread." Food, the greatest sustenance of nations, empires, ages gone, and ages to come. For those who grow food give them therefore their dues in equal appreciation as the man who plants a rig of steel that in years will decay. Everyone shares this common need for food and it makes us all equal. Let us remember therefore this principle in our machines of government.[23]

Universal proof of the wisdom of Sowande's choice may become more evident if we were to ask ourselves how the preceding statement might be received today by the farmers of middle America.

NOTES

CHAPTER FOUR

1
    Chinua Achebe and Cyprian Ekwensi have been
Nigeria's leading novelists since the sixties. Both men
enjoy well-deserved international reputations.

2
    Berth Lindfors, "Interview with Kole Omotoso." In
his DEM-SAY: INTERVIEWS WITH EIGHT NIGERIAN WRITERS.
Austin: African and Afro-American Studies and Research
Center, University of Texas, 1974, p. 55.

3
    References to Euba's portrayal of Lalunkle can be
found in Gerald Moore's WOLE SOYINKA (New York: Africana,
1971). His portrayal of Colonel Moses in 1977 was highly
praised by Shola Olaoye, Yoruba production consultant.

4
    Kole Omotoso, SHADOWS IN THE HORIZON (Ibadan:
Sketch Publishing Co. Ltd., 1977),p. 32.

5
    Lindfors, p. 52.

6
    Omotoso, pp. 35-36.

7
    Lindfors, p. 49.

8
    Femi Euba, THE GULF, 1983, Xerox, n.d., p. 65.

9
    Ibid., p. 12.

10
    Ibid., p. 64.

11
    Ibid., p. 71.

12
    Ibid., pp. 81-82.

13
    Ibid., pp. 75-76.

[14]
Bode Sowande,   FAREWELL TO BABYLON AND OTHER PLAYS (Washington, D.C.: Continents Press, 1979), p. 7.

[15]
Ibid., p. 59.

[16]
Ibid., p. 19.

[17]
Ibid., p. 7.

[18]
Ibid, p. 25.

[19]
Ibid., p. 68.

[20]
Ibid., pp. 126-27.

[21]
Ibid., p. 83.

[22]
Ibid., p. 76.

[23]
Ibid., p. 95.

CONCLUSION

An obvious conclusion that can be drawn from the preceding study is that the thoughts, ideas, and concerns of the playwrights are not alien to western interests. Soyinka's condemnation of political greed and social decimation must be applauded by all civilized human beings. Equally admirable is Rotimi's desire to remind us all of what is best in traditional society and the pressing need to preserve it. The almost cynical warnings from Omotoso, Euba, and Sowande should serve to remind us that we must all be vigilant in a world of egocentrism and terrorism to which none of us are immune.

None of the plays discussed are as much as thirty years old. A theatre as young as the Yoruba English Theatre may have yet to produce its greatest works. This should be a most exciting and reassuring fact when we consider the stature and sophistication of many of the works that have already been produced in the past two decades or so. It would appear that the Yoruba English Theatre holds, perhaps, the greatest promise of aiding in the production of an African theatrical tradition equal to any in the world. It is already offering to the West a rich and vital dramatic form that possesses many of the dramatic elements that are considered valuable but are often absent in today's western theatre. The organic ease with which we see the blending of dance, music, song and compendious ideas should make these dramas welcome and sought after in the west.

As part of a relatively new form of theatre, the Yoruba dramas in English are still searching for an acceptable identity all their own. Though some of the playwrights, Rotimi in particular, are making a conscious and concerted effort, the final product probably will be the result of a natural evolutionary process. The vitality and energy displayed by the playwrights is encouraging. They have all, to varying degrees, accomplished what Adrian Roscoe attributes to Soyinka.

They have taken "a body of religious belief, the dance, chants, songs, and ritual--and fused them with the most useful elements that western dramatists have to offer in regard to stage-craft, dramatic structure, characterization, and physical presentation. [1]

A desirable result of the dramatic activity described in chapter one would be the motivation of other Africans to study drama as a discipline and to write both plays and criticism. This would ensure that the best possible African theatre would be produced by those most qualified to produce it. Such a body of research and criticism would make studies such as this one and future research much easier and more fruitful.

A synthesis of findings for this study reveals, first of all, that the production of Yoruba drama in English can be accomplished without fear of the unfamiliar. The study also provides bibliographical information on both general and specialized studies on the Yoruba and their drama. It further demonstrates, through actual execution, a method of analysis that is thorough and easy to apply. In addition, the study contains fifteen plays which have been analyzed and

clarified. The knowledge gained through the clarification
of the Yoruba content, or sentiment, of these works will
aid greatly in the analysis of other Yoruba dramas.

At this point it may be helpful to discuss the
availability of texts. Though this study may serve as an
introduction to Yoruba drama for some, there is no
substitute for the scripts themselves. For those totally
unfamiliar with Yoruba or any other African Drama,
finding a point at which to start a search for scripts
might be a confusing task.

One of the first considerations should be the amount
of time available. If the production dates are far enough
in the future as to allow for thorough research, a plan
of attack can be formulated that will more often than
not result in success. If, however, there is time for
little more than the bear production cycle, consideration
might be given to employing a consultant. Professional
consultation is seldom free. Fees vary greatly, but are
often negotiable. Also, as will be shown later,
consultants can provide services other than those which
are directly related to the production such as community
relations.

There are other avenues available in addition to or
in lieu of professional consultation. Again, the choices
made will depend on the availability of time and scripts.
Anyone desiring to obtain copies of Soyinka's works
should have no trouble at all. He is very well published
in this country. Scripts and production information can
be obtained through normal channels. [2] Other playwrights
will present more of a problem.

The easiest and most obvious course of action is
library visitation. The card catalogue of most libraries
will lead you to only the works of the best-known and
most popular African authors. A more prudent use of time
might be to turn to indexes and bibliographies. [3]

For those who live in or near larger cities there

are bookstores which specialize in Black and African works. Of particular interest to producers in small towns would be a listing of these stores which is published periodically by THE BLACK SCHOLAR magazine in its BLACK BOOKS ROUND-UP editions. [4]

If the books being sought have not been published in this country, a very helpful agency would be The African Imprint Service. It is an extremely dependable organization with operatives in virtually every major African city. Subscribers to the service are allowed to request works in their particular areas of interest. The areas may be as broad or as narrow as the subscriber wishes. The service cannot guarantee time of delivery nor is it inexpensive. The fee for a play script or work of criticism is often as much as five times the item's cover price. [5]

A much cheaper purchasing service, though far less dependable, might be provided by friends or acquaintances who are African or who often visit Africa. If there is a university nearby it may be possible to obtain this service even if no such friends exist. Many universities with large numbers of African students very often have African student organizations. If contacted many of the students would be happy to check bookstores and libraries in their hometowns. The cost of purchasing and shipping would be required.

A final alternative, and virtually the only method of obtaining unpublished works, is to contact the playwrights themselves. The majority of the playwrights included in this study corresponded with me and agreed to help as much as their busy lives would allow. [6]

Obtaining texts might prove a bit difficult in some instances, but with a little perseverance and ingenuity most searches will be successful.

Having discussed the acquisition of texts we should now look briefly at the current degree to which Yoruba and other African productions are done in America. As with the availability of his plays, it is Soyinka who leads in the efforts at establishing Yoruba drama in America. Several of his plays have had their premiere performances in this country. [7]

Fortunately, it appears that, in recent years, African plays have begun to lose some of their exotic appeal and are being judged more on their merit as works of dramatic art. This has, with the possible exception of Athol Fugard's South African drama, made the professional production of African drama less profitable. [8]

For this reason the majority of the productions of Yoruba and other African dramas are to be found on university campuses and in smaller experimental theatres. This state of affairs is by no means cause for despair. American universities have historically played an important role in the development and promotion of non-traditional as well as traditional drama. The continued creation of university courses and departments of African study are helping to ensure the existence of a worthwhile body of art.

There are many practical ways of promoting interest in Yoruba theatre being employed by those who see the merits of the works. One example is the use made of the Yoruba consultant hired by the NCCU production staff of Soyinka's DEATH AND THE KING'S HORSEMAN. In addition to work on the production itself, the consultant agreed to conduct workshops not only for university students, but also for high school and elementary school students as well as the surrounding community at large.

As with all other drama the principal instrument of promotion for Yoruba drama will be the productions themselves. If they are done with the care and concern that should be employed in all productions, an increasingly stable future should be assured.

NOTES

CONCLUSION

1
   Adrian Roscoe, MOTHER IS GOLD(New York: Cambridge
University Press, 1971), p. 219.

2
   The majority of Soyinka's plays were published in
this country by the Oxford University Press. Exceptions
are OPERA WONYOSI, Indiana University press and DEATH AND
THE KING'S HORSEMAN, Eyre Methuen.

3
   Not all indexes and bibliographies are current
enough to be really helpful. Three of the best are J.O.
Asamani's INDEX AFRICANUS, Claudia Baldwin's NIGERIAN
LITERATURE: A BIBLIOGRAPHY OF CRITICISM, 1952-1976, and
David and Charlene Baldwin's THE YORUBA OF SOUTHWESTERN
NIGERIA: AN INDEXED BIBLIOGRAPHY. A more complete listing
can be found in June Balisteri's 1978 dissertation, THE
TRADITIONAL ELEMENTS OF THE YORUBA ALARINJO THEATRE IN
WOLE SOYINKA'S PLAYS.

4
   This publication not only lists bookstores, it also
provides a listing of publishers who specialize in Black
and African works as well as a listing of current works
complete with commentary and prices.

5
   The African Imprint Service is located at Box 350,
West Falmouth, MA 02574.

6
   All of the playwrights included in this study,with
the exception of Bode Sowande, were connected with the
Department of Dramatic art at the University of Ife.
Sowande should be contacted through the Odu Themes drama
group in Ibadan.

7
   Soyinka's American premieres have included MADMEN
AND SPECIALISTS at the O'Neil Theatre Center in 1970 and
A PLAY OF GIANTS at the Yale Repertory Theatre in 1984.
Soyinka has also done work with KONGI'S HARVEST in
America, including a film.

8

The recent New York success of Fugard's MASTER
HAROLD AND THE BOYS may be due, in part, to the
continuing concern that exists over South African
Apartheid.

APPENDIX

APPENDIX   A

YORUBA   TRANSLATIONS

Following   are   translations   of   the   Yoruba   chants,
songs, and phrases found in Kole Omotoso's SHADOWS IN THE
HORIZON. The   translations were   provided by Mr. Lucky T.
Osho and follow each section of Yoruba dialogue. The page
numbers   are   from   the   1977   edition   of SHADOWS IN THE
HORIZON printed by the Sketch publishing company, Ibadan.

page 19-

(From off-stage   right a   procession of   Aladura is heard
singing)

    E ba mi gbe Jesu ga BaBa
    E ba mi gbe Jesu ga Omo
    Eni tio ba gba Jesu lo l'Oluwa
    E ba mi gbe Jesu ga.

    Help me praise Jesus the Father
    Help me praise Jesus the Son
    Whoever accepts Christ as God
    Help me praise   Jesus.

Aladura Leader: Mo ti mo pelese ni mi
                  Oluwa dariji mo o
A Woman: Mo ti mo pasewo ni mi
                  Olorun dariji mi o
Businessman: Mo to mo pe olowo ni mi
                  Ara wa dariji mi o

150

Securityman: MO ti mo pelewon ni mi
                       Oku orun dariji mi o
Professor: Mo ti mo professor ni mi
                       Iwe mi dariji mi o

I know I am a sinner
God forgive me
I know I an a prostitute
God forgive me
I know I am a rich man
Body forgive me
I know I am a prisoner
May the spirit forgive me
I know I am a professor
may my books forgive me

Professor: E yo ninu Oluwa e yo
E yo e fope fagbara re
E yo
E yo
E yo ninu Oluwa e yo

Bawo ni ng o se dolowo
Ti gbogbo aiye yio je temi?
E yo
E yo
E yo ninu Oluwa e yo.

Be happy in the Lord, be happy
Be happy and glory in his power
Be happy
Be happy
Be happy in the Lord, be happy

How can I be a rich person
And the whole world be mine?

                    Be happy
                    Be happy
                    Be happy in the Lord, be happy

page 20-

Aladura Leader:
WO 'le niwaju Oluwa, ki o si fi ohun rara bere
owo lowo Re!

(The professor kneels down and the Aladura leader puts
his hand on him)

Olorun Omo, Olorun Baba, Olorun Emi Mimo.
Awa omo re Alailowo lowo ke pe o
Wa, fun wa lowo Amin.
Olorun okuta meta ti Dafidi fi san pese Golayati,
Awa ke pe O, fun wa lowo
Fun arakunrin wa yi professor lowo
Ki o ra moto lori moto; ki o kole lori ile
Ki o ra'le lo yanturu.
Olorun kan losan ati loru
Olowo gbogborogbo ti nde gbogbo banki
Kowo fun wa! Kowo fun wa!
Jeki owo pe lowo wa!
Jeki owo pe lapo wa!
Gbogbo eyi ni a ntoro loruko Jesu
Asekanmaku!

Kneel before the Lord and ask for Riches!

(The Professor kneels down and the Aladura leader puts
his hand on him)
God the Son, the Father, and Holy Spirit

It is we your children that are calling you
Come, and give us money, Amen.
God that made it possible for David to kill Goliath with
a piece of stone,
We call unto you, to give us money.
Give this our professor riches
To be able to buy a fleet of cars; and houses upon
houses.
For him to buy endless lands
Our God in the afternoon and night with hands long enough
to reach all banks
Give us money! Give us money!
Let the money stay longer with us!
Let the money stay longer in our pockets!
All this we ask in the name of Jesus
Forever and ever!

(The professor rises; the Aladura Leader demands money
for the prayers, and the Professor bursts into song).

Professor: Jesu ko gbo 'wo
                  Jesu ko gbo 'wo
                  Jesu ko gbo 'wo lowo enikan
                  Alleluyah!!!

                  O ti femire ra wa
                  O ti femire ra wa
                  O ti femire ra wa lowo iku
                  Alleluyah!!!

                  Jesus received no money
                  Jesus received no money
                  Jesus received no money from anybody
                  Hallelujah!!!

His death has saved us
His death has saved us
He has saved us from death
Hallelujah!!!

page 33-

(The old woman comes in clutching her letter which she now profers to Citizen Judge).

Old Woman: E jowo e de ba mi wo jwe me yi wo.
       Please, kindly help me read this letter.

(Bibilari takes the letter and reads):

  Mama mi owon,
   Pelu ayo ati alafia ni mo fi ko iwe mi yi si yin.
Se alafia ni e wa o.
   Nipa oro owo ti e so ninu iwe yin ti mo ri gba,
emi yio fi naria kan ati adoota kobo ranse si yin ni
ipari osu yi o.
   Ki e ba mi ki baba mi ati awon anti mi oro mi ko
ju bayi lo.

      Emi ni omo yin.
      Clement Bamigbade.

Dear Mother,

     I am writing with joy and in good health, hope you are fine. Concerning the money you talked about in your letter that I received. I will, send a dollar and thirty cents to you at the end of the month.

     Kindly extend my greetings to my father and sisters.

Yours Sincerely,
Clement Bamigbade

     The following phrases are very short and can be translated out of context with no danger of mis-interpretation.

page 35-

     Ki le nf'Oba pe
     Oba o, Oba lase, Oba!

     What do you call the king to be
     King, King, the commander, King!

page 36-

     Atowo atomo
     Mofe be!

     Both money and children
     I'd like to have

page 37-

A o soyinbo Yes
Ao sodewa Aree

We speak in English Yes
We speak in our language Aree

page 40-

Eyin ni yen? E kaa san. Mo dupe. Ki le ti wi?

Is that you? Good afternoon. I am grateful. What did you say?

page 41-

Nwon mba mi soro ni bi ni. En-hen.
Ejow

He was talking to me.
Please

page 42-

lafia ko? lafia kalau.

How are you? I am alright.

awa dobale o!

I am prostrate!

APPENDIX B

INTERVIEWS, REVIEWS, and CRITICISM

The following interviews, reviews, and criticisms were selected from Claudia Baldwin's book, NIGERIAN LITERATURE: A BIBLIOGRAPHY OF CRITICISM, 1952-1976. Baldwin's book is a compilation of criticism of the fiction, poetry, and drama written by fifty-one Nigerian authors in English.

Because interviews and reviews are extremely helpful in production research I have separated and placed them into this appendix. As a rule interviews and reviews tend to yield production insights much quicker than more formal criticism and commentary.

Interviews and Reviews
Kole Omotoso

Agetua,John. "Interview with Kole Omotoso." In his INTERVIEWS WITH SIX NIGERIAN WRITERS. Benin City: Bendel Newspapers Corp., 1976, pp. 10-16.

Bozimo, Willy. "Dr. Omotoso: Novelist and Academician. SPEAR, July 1976, pp. 35-36.

Dohan, Oyado. "Kole Omotoso in Review." INDIGO, 2, No.1 (March 1975), 14, 16, 18-19.

----------"Kole Omotoso" AFRICAN BOOK PUBLISHING RECORD, 2, No. 1 (January 1976), 12-14.

"Interview with Wole Soyinka." CULTURAL EVENTS IN AFRICA (18 MAY 1966), 2-12.

Lindfors, Bernth. "Kole Omotoso Interviewed by Bernth Lindfors in Ibadan, May 14, 1973." CULTURAL EVENTS IN AFRICA, No. 103 (1975), 2-12.

Walder, Dennis."Interview with Kole Omotoso." TRANSITION, 9, No. 44 (1974), 45-57.

THE COMBAT--Reviews

Conateh, Swaebou. NDAANAN, 4, Nos. 1-2 (March/September 1974), 64-65.

Iheakaram, Paul O. AFRISCOPE, 4, No. 4 (April 1974), 49.

THE EDIFICE--Reviews

AFRISCOPE, 4, No. 3 (March 1974), 47-49.

CHOICE, 9, No. 11 (January 1973), 1453.

Conateh, Swaebou. NDAANAN, 4, Nos. 1-2 (March/September 1974), 64-65.

W., D. "Passing Through." WEST AFRICA, No. 2912, (April 1973), 436.

SACRIFICE--Review

Akobi, Kofi. AFRISCOPE, 5, No. 8 (August 1975), 53, 55.

Interviews and Reviews
Ola Rotimi

Asein, Samuel Omo. "Ola Rotimi and the New Dramatic Movement at Ife." BULLENTIN OF BLACK THEATRE, 1, No. 2 (Winter 1972), 4-5.

Folarin, M. "Ola Rotimi Interviewed." NEW THEATRE MAGAZINE, 12, No. 2 (1972), 5-7.

Lindfors, Bernth. "Interview with Ola Rotimi." In his DEM-SAY: INTERVIEWS WITH EIGHT NIGERIAN WRITERS. Austin: African and Afro-American Studies and Research Center, University of Texas, 1974, pp. 57-68.

Wren, Robert M. "Ola Rotimi: A Major New Talent." AFRICA REPORT, 18, No. 5 (Sept-Oct. 1973), 29-31.

THE GODS ARE NOT TO BLAME--Reviews

Bishop, Terry. "African Oedipus." WEST AFRICA, No. 2850, (Jan. 1972), 97.

Rendle, Adrian. DRAMA, no. 103 (Winter 1971), 77.

THE GODS ARE NOT TO BLAME--Reviews of Production

Adelugba, Dapo. IBADAN, No. 27 (Oct. 1969), 49-50.

Badejo, Peter. "Premier Production: THE GODS ARE NOT TO BLAME." AFRICAN ARTS/ARTS d'AFRIQUE, 3, No. 2 (Winter 1970), 64-65.

KURUNMI--Review

Rendle, Adrian. DRAMA, No. 108 (Spring 1973), 82-84.

KURUNMI--Review of Production

Oke, Ola. "Tragedy Beautifully Rendered." NIGERIA MAGAZINE, No. 102, Sept.-Nov. 1969, pp. 525-27.

OVONRAMWEN NOGBAISI--Review of Production

Asein,Samuel O. "The Tragic Grandeur of OVONRAMWEN NOGBAISI." NIGERIA MAGAZINE, Nos. 110-12, 1974, pp. 40-49.

THE PRODIGAL--Review of Production

Ajolore, O. "Last Evening at Ori Olokun." NIGERIA MAGAZINE, No. 102, Sept.-Nov. 1969, pp. 528-29.

Interviews and Reviews
Wole Soyinka

Agetua, John. "Interview with Wole Soyinka." In his INTERVIEWS WITH SIX NIGERIAN WRITERS. Benin City: Bendel Newspapers Corp., 1976, pp. 38-57.

Gates, Louis S. "An Interview with Soyinka." BLACK WORLD, 24, No.10 (Aug. 1975), 30-48.

Jeyifous, Biodun. "Wole Soyinka." TRANSITION, 8, No. 2, (1973), 62-64.

Mphahlele, Exekiel. "Wole Soyinka." In AFRICAN WRITERS TALKING. Ed. by C. Pieterse and D. Duerden. New York: Africana, 1972, pp. 171-77.

THE BACCHAE OF EURIPIDES--Reviews

BOOKLIST, 71, No. 9, 1Jan. 1975, p. 439.

CHOICE, 11, No. 12, Feb. 1975, p. 1772.

Knox, Bernard. "Greek for the Greekless." NEW YORK REVIEW OF BOOKS, 23, No.1, 5 Feb. 1976, pp. 11-12.

LUDDY, THOMAS E. LIBRARY JOURNAL, 100, No. 1, 1 Jan. 1975, p. 62.

"Myth-Mesh." TIMES LITERARY SUPPLEMENT, 1 Mar. 1974, p.214.

THE BACCHAE OF EURIPIDES--Review of Production

Lahr, John. PLAYS AND PLAYERS, 21, No. 1, (Oct. 1973), 59.

THE BACCHAE OF EURIPIDES--Criticism

Bibbs, James. "Brook in Nigeria: Soyinka in London." ODU, 1, No. 3, Oct. 1973, pp. 16-19.

COLLECTED PLAYS, I--Reviews

BOOKLIST, 70, No. 15, 1 Apr. 1974, p. 850

CHOICE, 11, Nos. 5-6, July-Aug. 1974, p.768.

Rendle, Adrian. DRAMA, No. 111, Winter 1973, pp. 87-88.

COLLECTED   PLAYS   II--Reviews

AFRISCOPE, 5, No. 8, Aug. 1975, p. 55.

Coleby, John. DRAMA, No. 116, Spring 1975, pp. 91-93.

A DANCE OF THE FOREST--Reviews

Banham, Martin.   BOOKS ABROAD, 38, No. 1, Winter 1964, p. 92.

Beier, Ulli. BLACK ORPHEUS, No. 8 (1960), 5758.

Blair, D.S. ENGLISH   STUDIES IN AFRICA, 7, No. 1 (Mar. 1964), 128-31.

Holmes, Timothy.   "Five Soyinka Plays."   THE NEW AFRICAN, 2, No. 6 (July 1963), 112-13.

A DANCE OF THE FOREST--Reviews of Production

Bare. AFRICAN HORIZON, No. 2, Jan. 1961, pp. 8-11.

Cockshott, Una. IBADAN, No. 10, Nov. 1960, pp. 30-32.

A DANCE OF THE FOREST--Criticism

Gaston, Jessie. "A Dance of the Forests: A Critique. BUSARA, 7, No. 1 (1975), 33-40.

Gibbs, James.   "The Origins of A Dance of the Forests." AFRICAN LITERATURE TODAY, No. 8 (1976), 66-71.

Gleason, Judith.   "Out of the Irony of Words." TRANSITION,4, No. 18 (1965), 34-38.

Watson, Ian. "Soyinka's Dance of the Forests." TRANSITION, 6, No. 27 (1966), 24-26.

Wilkinson, Nick. "Demoke's Choice in Soyinka's A DANCE OF THE FOREST." JOURNAL OF COMMONWEALTH LITERATURE, 10, No. 3 (Apr. 1976), 22-27.

DEATH AND THE KING'S HORSEMAN--Reviews

Banham, Martin. "New Soyinka Play." JOURNAL OF COMMONWEALTH LITERATURE, 10, No. 3 (Apr. 1976), 80-81.

BOOKLIST, 72, No. 20, 15 June 1976, pp. 1443-44.

CHOICE, 13, No. 7, Sept. 1976, p. 837.

Coleby, John. DRAMA, No. 119, Winter 1975, p. 87.

Hale, Thomas A. LIBRARY JOURNAL, 101, No. 10, 15 May 1976, p. 1222.

Jones, D.A.N. "This World and the Next." TIMES LITERARY SUPPLEMENT, (17 Oct. 1975), p. 1238.

FIVE PLAYS--Reviews

CHOICE, 2, No. 12, Feb. 1966, p. 870.

Hill, Geoffrey. "Nigerian Plays." JOURNAL OF COMMONWEALTH LITERATURE, No. 1 (Sept. 1965), 172-74.

Jones, D.A.N. NEW STATESMAN, 69, No. 1768, 29 Jan. 1965, p. 164.

"Third World Stage." TIMES LITERARY SUPPLEMENT, (1 Apr. 1965), p. 252.

Wright, Edgar. EAST AFRICA JOURNAL, 2, No. 7 (Nov. 1965), 35-36, 38.

Yankowitz, Susan. "The plays of Wole Soyinka." AFRICAN FORUM, 1, No. 4 (Spring 1966), 129-33.

FIVE PLAYS--Criticism

Elate, Mike E. "The Intellectual as an Artist in Soyinka's FIVE PLAYS." In MELANGES AFRICAINS. Yaounde: Editions Pedagogiques Afrique-Contact, 1973, pp. 299-327.

Esslin, Martin. "Two African Playwrights." BLACK ORPHEUS, No. 19 (March 1966), 33-39.

THE JERO PLAYS--Reviews

"The Battle of the Beach." TIMES LITERARY SUPPLEMENT, (8 Feb. 1974), 138.

Gibbs, J. BOOKS ABROAD, 48, No. 4, Autumn 1974, pp. 834-35.

Mellors, John. LONDON MAGAZINE, 14, No. 1, Apr.-May 1974, pp. 135-36.

KONGI'S HARVEST--Reviews

Arden, John. NEW THEATRE MAGAZINE, 12, No. 2, 1972, pp. 25-26.

164

Banham, Martin. "Nigerian Dramatists." JOURNAL OF
COMMONWEALTH LITERATURE, No. 7 (July 1969), 132-36.

Dipoko, Mbella Sonne. PRESCENCE AFRICAINE, No.63, 1967,
pp. 262-63.

Thorpe, Michael. ENGLISH STUDIES, 49,No. 3, June 1968, p.
275.

W., K. WEST AFRICA, No. 2609, 3 June 1967, pp. 723, 725.

KONGI'S HARVEST--Reviews of Production

Berry, Boyd M. IBADAN, No. 23, Oct. 1966, pp. 53-55.

Clurman, Harold. THE NATION, 206, No. 18, Apr. 1968, p.
581.

Dathrone, O.R. BLACK ORPHEUS, No. 21, Apr. 1967, pp.
60-61.

Kerr, Walter. "Tantalizing but Blurred." NEW YORK
TIMES, (21 Apr. 1968), 93.

Kroll, Jack. "Caesar in Africa." NEWSWEEK, 71, No. 18 (29
Apr. 1968), 93.

Lew, Theophilus. AMERICA, 118, No. 19, May 1968, pp.
651-52.

Oke, Ola. "Tragedy Beautifully Rendered." NIGERIA
MAGAZINE, No. 102, Sept.-Nov. 1969, pp. 525-27.

Oliver, Edith. THE NEW YORKER, 44, No. 10, Apr. 1968, pp.
86, 91.

Sullivan, Dan. "Confrontation in a Tribe." NEW YORK
TIMES, (15 Apr. 1968), 49.

KONGI'S HARVEST--Criticism

Atilade, David. "KONGI'S HARVEST, and the Men Who Made
the Film." INTERLINK, 6, No. 4 (Oct.-Dec. 1970), 4-14.

Brown, Nigel. NOTES ON WOLE SOYINKA'S KONGI'S HARVEST.
Nairobi: Heinemann Educational Books, 1973.
Gibbs, James. STUDY AID TO KONGI'S HARVEST. London: Rex
Collings 1973.

Larson, Charles R. "Nigerian Drama Comes of Age." AFRICA
REPORT, 13, No. 5 (May 1968), 55-57.

Mbughuni, P. "A GRAIN OF WHEAT, SONG OF LAWINO, SONG OF
OCOL, and KONGI'S HARVEST." UMMA, 5, No. 1 (1975), 64-74.

Mshengu."KONGI'S HARVEST by Wole Soyinka." S'KETSH',
(Summer 1973), 33-34.

THE LION AND THE JEWEL--Reviews

Banham, Martin. BOOKS ABROAD, 38, No. 1, Winter 1964, p.
92.

Blair, D.S. ENGLISH STUDIES IN AFRICA, 7, No. 1, Mar.
1964, pp. 128-31.

Green, Robert. "The Clashing Old and New." THE NATION,
201, No.11 (11 Oct. 1965), 224-25.

Holmes, Timothy. "Five Soyinka Plays." THE NEW AFRICAN, 2, No. 6 (13 July 1963), 112-13.

Kunene, Mazisi and Cosmo Pieterse. "Soyinka in London: Two Writers in London Asses THE LION AND THE JEWEL." THE NEW AFRICAN, 6, No. 1 (Mar.1967), 9-10.

Nazareth, Peter. Transition, 4, No. 10, Sept. 1963, pp. 47-48.

THE LION AND THE JEWEL--Reviews of Production

Akanji, Sangodare. "Criticism of THE LION AND THE JEWEL and THE SWAMP DWELLERS." BLACK ORPHEUS, No.6 (Nov. 1959), 50-51.

Banjo, Ayo. "THE LION AND THE JEWEL at the Arts Theatre." IBADAN, No. 26 (Feb. 1969), 82-83.

Bryden, Ronald. "African Sophistication." THE OBSERVER (18 Dec. 1966), 20.

Darlington, W.A. "Single Parable of African Life." THE DAILY TELEGRAPH (13 Dec. 1966), 15.

Hobson, Harold. "The Lion And the Jewel from Africa." CHRISTAIN SCIENCE MONITOR (6 Jan. 1967), 4.

Jones, D.A.N. NEW STATESMAN, 72, No. 1866, 16 Dec. 1966, p. 916.

Ngugi, James. TRANSITION, 3, No. 12, Jan.-Feb. 1964, p. 55.

"Nigerian Play for Court Theatre." THE TIMES, 28 Nov. 1966, p. 6.

"Sheer Igenuity of Soyinka's Plot." THE TIMES, 13 Dec. 1966, p. 6.

S'KETSH', Summer 1974-75, pp. 36-37.

Taylor, John Russell. "Avoiding the Insulting." PLAYS AND PLAYERS, 14, No. 5 (Feb.1967), 14-15.

THE LION AND THE JEWEL--Criticism

Erapu, Laban. NOTES ON WOLE SOYINKA'S THE LION AND THE JEWEL. Nairobi: Heinemann Educational Books, 1976.

Kronenfeld, J.Z. "The Communalistic African and the Individualistic Westerner: Some Comments on Misleading Generalizations in Western Criticism of Soyinka and Achebe." RESEARCH IN AFRICAN LITERATURES, 6, No. 2 (Fall 1975), 199-225.

Mcelroy, Hilda. "Some Stylistic Expressions, Attitudes and Patterns in Contemporary African Drama." THE PAN AFRICANIST, No. 3 (Dec. 1971), 39-41.

Mohmed, A. "THE LION AND THE JEWEL Reconsidered: Observations on the Relation between Character and Language in the Play." THE MIRROR (1972-73), 34-41.

Povey, John F. "Wole Soyinka: Two Nigerian Comedies." COMPARATIVE DRAMA, 3, No. 2 (Summer 1969), 120-32.

Taiow, Oladele. "Wole Soyinka: THE LION AND THE JEWEL." In his AN INTRODUCTION TO WEST AFRICAN LITERATURE. london: Nelson, 1967, pp. 163-76.

Taueman, Howard. "A Nigerian Looks at 'Progress.'" NEW YORK TIMES (18 Apr. 1965), II, p. 1.

Walker, Bill. "Mime in THE LION AND THE JEWEL." WORLD LITERATURE WRITTEN IN ENGLISH, 12, No. 1. (Apr. 1973), 37-44.

MADMEN AND SPECIALISTS--Reviews

AB BOOKMAN'S WEEKLY, 49 19 June 1972, p. 2331.

"Anti-War Play." LITERARY HALF-YEARLY, 14, No. 1 Jan. 1973, pp. 166-68.

Banham, Martin. "Darkness and Threat." JOURNAL OF COMMONWEALTH LITERATURE, 8, No. 1 (June 1973), 124-26.

Calder, Angus. NEW STATESMAN, 83, No. 2145, 28 Apr. 1972, p. 564.

CHOICE, 9, No. 11, Jan. 1973, p. 1454.

"The Devotees of As." TIMES LITERARY SUPPLEMENT (31 Dec. 1971), p. 1632.

Menkiti, Ifeanyi. LITERARY JOURNAL, 97, No. 15 (Sept. 1972), 2748.

Rendle, Adrian. DRAMA, No. 104, Spring 1972, p. 81.

W., K. "Soyinka Before and After." WEST AFRICA, No. 2868 (2 June 1972), 692-93.

MADMEN AND SPECIALISTS--Reviews of Production

Green, Robert. "The Clashing Old and New." THE NATION, 201, No.11 (11 Oct. 1965), 224-25.

Holmes, Timothy. "Five Soyinka Plays." THE NEW AFRICAN, 2, No. 6 (13 July 1963), 112-13.

Kunene, Mazisi and Cosmo Pieterse. "Soyinka in London: Two Writers in London Asses THE LION AND THE JEWEL." THE NEW AFRICAN, 6, No. 1 (Mar.1967), 9-10.

Nazareth, Peter. Transition, 4, No. 10, Sept. 1963, pp. 47-48.

THE LION AND THE JEWEL--Reviews of Production

Akanji, Sangodare. "Criticism of THE LION AND THE JEWEL and THE SWAMP DWELLERS." BLACK ORPHEUS, No.6 (Nov. 1959), 50-51.

Banjo, Ayo. "THE LION AND THE JEWEL at the Arts Theatre." IBADAN, No. 26 (Feb. 1969), 82-83.

Bryden, Ronald. "African Sophistication." THE OBSERVER (18 Dec. 1966), 20.

Darlington, W.A. "Single Parable of African Life." THE DAILY TELEGRAPH (13 Dec. 1966), 15.

Hobson, Harold. "The Lion And the Jewel from Africa." CHRISTAIN SCIENCE MONITOR (6 Jan. 1967), 4.

Jones, D.A.N. NEW STATESMAN, 72, No. 1866, 16 Dec. 1966, p. 916.

Ngugi, James. TRANSITION, 3, No. 12, Jan.-Feb. 1964, p. 55.

"Nigerian Play for Court Theatre." THE TIMES, 28 Nov. 1966, p. 6.

"Sheer Igenuity of Soyinka's Plot." THE TIMES, 13 Dec. 1966, p. 6.

S'KETSH', Summer 1974-75, pp. 36-37.

Taylor, John Russell. "Avoiding the Insulting." PLAYS AND PLAYERS, 14, No. 5 (Feb.1967), 14-15.

THE LION AND THE JEWEL--Criticism

Erapu, Laban. NOTES ON WOLE SOYINKA'S THE LION AND THE JEWEL. Nairobi: Heinemann Educational Books, 1976.

Kronenfeld, J.Z. "The Communalistic African and the Individualistic Westerner: Some Comments on Misleading Generalizations in Western Criticism of Soyinka and Achebe." RESEARCH IN AFRICAN LITERATURES, 6, No. 2 (Fall 1975), 199-225.

Mcelroy, Hilda. "Some Stylistic Expressions, Attitudes and Patterns in Contemporary African Drama." THE PAN AFRICANIST, No. 3 (Dec. 1971), 39-41.

Mohmed, A. "THE LION AND THE JEWEL Reconsidered: Observations on the Relation between Character and Language in the Play." THE MIRROR (1972-73), 34-41.

Povey, John F. "Wole Soyinka: Two Nigerian Comedies." COMPARATIVE DRAMA, 3, No. 2 (Summer 1969), 120-32.

Taiow, Oladele. "Wole Soyinka: THE LION AND THE JEWEL." In his AN INTRODUCTION TO WEST AFRICAN LITERATURE. london: Nelson, 1967, pp. 163-76.

Taueman, Howard. "A Nigerian Looks at 'Progress.'" NEW YORK TIMES (18 Apr. 1965), II, p. 1.

Walker, Bill. "Mime in THE LION AND THE JEWEL." WORLD LITERATURE WRITTEN IN ENGLISH, 12, No. 1. (Apr. 1973), 37-44.

MADMEN AND SPECIALISTS--Reviews

AB BOOKMAN'S WEEKLY, 49 19 June 1972, p. 2331.

"Anti-War Play." LITERARY HALF-YEARLY, 14, No. 1 Jan. 1973, pp. 166-68.

Banham, Martin. "Darkness and Threat." JOURNAL OF COMMONWEALTH LITERATURE, 8, No. 1 (June 1973), 124-26.

Calder, Angus. NEW STATESMAN, 83, No. 2145, 28 Apr. 1972, p. 564.

CHOICE, 9, No. 11, Jan. 1973, p. 1454.

"The Devotees of As." TIMES LITERARY SUPPLEMENT (31 Dec. 1971), p. 1632.

Menkiti, Ifeanyi. LITERARY JOURNAL, 97, No. 15 (Sept. 1972), 2748.

Rendle, Adrian. DRAMA, No. 104, Spring 1972, p. 81.

W., K. "Soyinka Before and After." WEST AFRICA, No. 2868 (2 June 1972), 692-93.

MADMEN AND SPECIALISTS--Reviews of Production

Bunce, Alan. "Soyinka's Nigerian Play: Madmen and Specialists." CHRISTIAN SCIENCE MONITOR (15 Aug. 1970), 12.

Gussow, Mel. "Psychological Play from Nigeria." NEW YORK TIMES (3 Aug. 1970), p. 38.

MADMEN AND SPECIALISTS--Criticism

Bamikunle, Adermi. "What is 'As'? Why 'As'? A Thematic Exegesis of Wole Soyinka's MADMEN AND SPECIALISTS." WORK IN PROGRESS, 2 (1973), 126-49.

Berry, Boyd. "On Looking at MADMEN AND SPECIALISTS." PAN AFRICAN JOURNAL, 5, No. 4 (Winter 1972), 461-71.

Gussow, Mel. "The Making of a Play." TOPIC, No. 58 (1971), pp. 29-31.

Iyengar, K.R. Srinivasa. "Soyinka's Latest Play." LITERARY HALF-YEARLY, 17, No. 2 (July 1976), 3-17.

Johnson, Chris. "Performance and Role-Playing in Soyinka's MADMEN AND SPECIALISTS." JOURNAL OF COMMONWEALTH LITERATURE, 10, No. 3 (Apr. 1976), 27-33.

McCartney, Barney C. "Traditional Satire in Wole Soyinka's MADMEN AND SPECIALISTS." WORLD LITERATURE WRITTEN IN ENGLISH, 14, No. 2 (Nov. 1975), 506-13.

THE ROAD--Reviews

CHOICE, 3, Nos. 5-6, July-Aug. 1966, p. 423.

Duncan, Bernice G. BOOKS ABROAD, 40, No.3, Summer 1966, pp. 360-61.

"Keep Off the Road." TIMES LITERARY SUPPLEMENT (10 June 1965), p. 476.

Pieterse, Cosmo. "Dramatic Riches." JOURNAL OF COMMONWEALTH LITERATURE, No. 2. (Dec. 1966), 168-71.

Shelton, Austin Jesse, Jr. AFRICA REPORT, 11, No. 5 May 1966, p. 66.

Yankiwitz, Susan. "The Plays of Wole Soyinka." AFRICAN FORUM, 1, No. 4 (spring 1966), 129-33.

THE ROAD--Reviews of Production

Billington, Michael. "First Night." PLAYS AND PLAYERS, 13, No. 2 (Nov. 1965), 34.
Bryden, Ronald. "The Asphalt God." NEW STATESMAN, 70, No. 1802 (24 Sept. 1965), 460-61.

Fay, Gerald. THE GUARDIAN, 15 Sept. 1965, p. 7.

Gilliatt, Penelope. "A Nigerian Original." THE OBSERVER (19 Sept. 1965), 25.

Hobson, Harold. "Nigerian Drama in Premiere." CHRISTIAN SCIENCE MONITOR (22 Sept. 1965), 4.

M., J.A. "Clark & Soyinka at the Commonwealth Arts Festival." THE NEW AFRICAN, 4, No. 8 (Oct. 1965), 195.

Pieterse, Cosmo. CULTURAL EVENTS IN AFRICA, No. 10, Sept. 1965, pp. 4-5.

"Rambustious Start to Festival." THE TIMES (15 Sept. 1965), p. 14.

Serumaga, Robert. "THE ROAD, by Wole Soyinka: Reaction of the Critics." CULTURAL EVENTS IN AFRICA, No. 11 (Oct. 1965), Supplement pp. I-II.

Shorter, Eric. "Nigerian Author of Talent." THE DAILY TETEGRAPH (15 Sept. 1965). p. 18.

"Soyinka's Hard Road." THE OBSERVER (19 Sept. 1965), p.23.

Spurling, Hilary. THE SPECTATOR (24 Sept. 1965), p. 380.

WEST AFRICA, No. 2520, 18 Sept. 1965, p. 1061.

WEST AFRICA, No. 2523, 9 Oct. 1965, p. 1133.

THE ROAD--Criticism

Amankulor, James Nduka. "Dramatic Technique and Meaning in THE ROAD." BA SHIRU, 7, No. 1 (1976), 53-58.

Izevbaye, D.S. "Language and Meaning in Soyinka's THE ROAD." AFRICAN LITERATURE TODAY, No. 8 (1967), 52-65. Moyo, S. Phaniso. "THE ROAD, a Slice of the Yoruba Pantheon." BA SHIRU (Fall 1970-Spring 1971), 89-93.

THE STRONG BREED--Reviews of Production

Clurman, Harold. THE NATION, 205, No. 19, 4 Dec. 1967), p. 606.

"Infectious Humanity." TIME (17 Nov. 1967), pp. 50, 52.

Oliver, Edith. THE NEW YORKER, 43, No. 39 (18 Nov. 1967),133-34.

Wardle, Irving. "Clash of Values." THE TIMES (27 Nov. 1968), p. 8a.

Weales, Gerald. THE REPORTER, 38, No. 3, 8 Feb. 1968, pp. 39-40.

THE SWAMP DWELLERS--Review of Production

Akanji, Sangodare. BLACK ORPHEUS, No. 6 (Nov. 1959), 50-51.

THE SWAMP DWELLERS--Criticism

MacLean, Una, M.M. Mahood, and Phebean Ogundipe. "Three Views of 'The Swamp Dwellers.'" IBADAN, No. 6 (June 1959), 27-30.

THREE PLAYS--Reviews

Akanji. BLACK ORPHEUS, No. 13 (Nov. 1963), 58-59.

Banham, Martin. "Criticism of Soyinka's THREE PLAYS." BOOKS ABROAD, 38, No. 1 (Winter 1964), 92.

Cook, David. "Of the Strong Breed." TRANSITION, 3, No. 13 (Mar.-Apr. 1964), 38-40.

Holmes, Timothy. "Five Soyinka Plays." THE NEW AFRICAN, 2, No. 6 (13 July 1963), 112-13.

THE TRIALS OF BROTHER JERO--Reviews of Production

Clurman, Harold. NATION, 205, No. 19, 4 Dec. 1967, p. 606.

"Harsh Comedy on Lagos Beach." THE TIMES (29 June 1966), p. 7.

"Infectious Humanity." TIME (17 Nov. 1967), 50, 52.

Jones, D.A.N. NEW STATESMAN, 72, No. 1843, 8 July 1966, pp. 63-64.

MacLean, Una. "Three One-Act Plays." IBADAN, No. 9 (June 1960), 21.

Nagenda, John. CULTURAL EVENTS IN AFRICA, No. 20, July 1966, pp. III-IV.

Nwankwo, Nkem. NIGERIA MAGAZINE, No. 72, Mar. 1962, p. 80.

Oliver, Edith. NEW YORKER, 43, No. 39 (18 Nov. 1967), 133-34.

WEST AFRICA, No. 2916, 30 Apr. 1973, pp. 563-64.

THE TRIALS OF BROTHER JERO--Criticism

Jabbi, Bu-Buakei. "The Form of Discovery in BROTHER JERO." JOURNAL OF THE NIGERIAN ENGLISH STUDIES ASSOCIATION, 7, Nos. 1-2 (Dec. 1975), 43-50.

Povey, John. "Wole Soyinka: Two Nigerian Comedies."*lm25

COMPARATIVE DRAMA, 3, No. 2 (Summer 1969), 120-32.

Priebe, Richard. "Soyinka's Brother Jero: Prophet, Politician, and Trickster." PAN AFRICAN JOURNAL, 4, No.4 (Fall 1971), 431-39.

BIBLIOGRAPHY

ANTHROPOLOGICAL STUDIES ON THE YOURBA

Ajisafe, A.k. THE LAWS AND CUSTOMS OF THE YORUBA PEOPLE.
London: George Routledge & Sons, Ltd., 1924.

Bascom, William R. "The Principle of Seniorty in the
SocialStructure of the Yoruba." AMERICAN ANTHROPOLOGIST,
n.s., 44 (1928), 37-46.

----------"The Sanctions of Ifa Divination."
THE JOURNAL OF THE ROYAL ANTHROPOLOGICAL INSTITUTE OF
GREAT BRITAIN AND IRELAND, 71 (1941), 43-54.

----------"The Sociological Role of the Yoruba
Cult-Group." AMERICAN ANTHROPOLOGIST, 46 (1944), 54-71.

Beier, H.U."Festival of the Images." NIGERIA, 45 (1945)
14-20.

Clarke, J.D. "Ifa Divination." JOURNAL OF THE ROYAL
ANTHROPOLOGICAL INSTITUTE OF GREAT BRITAIN AND IRELAND,
79 (1959), 235-56.

Forde, Daryll. THE YORUBA-SPEAKING PEOPLES OF
SOUTH-WESTERN NIGERIA. London: International African
Institute, 1951.

Johnson, Samuel. THE HISTORY OF THE YORUBA FROM THE
EARLIEST TIMES TO THE BEGINNING OF THE BRITISH
PROTECTORATE. London: George Rutlrdge & Sons, Ltd., 1921.

LLoyd, Peter C. "The Yoruba of Nigeria." PEOPLES OF AFRICA. ed. James L. Gibbs, Jr. New York: Holt, rinehart and Winston, Inc., 1965.

----------"The Yoruba Lineage." AFRICA, (1955), 235-51.

----------"Craft Organizations in Yoruba Towns." AFRICA, 23(1953), 30-44.

----------"The Traditional Political System of the Yoruba." SOUTHWESTERN JOURNAL OF ANTHROPOLOGY, 10 (1954), 366-84.

----------"Yoruba Myths--A Sociologist's Interpretation." ODU, 2 (1955), 20-28.

Parrinder, Geoffrey. WEST AFRICAN RELIGION: ILLUSTRATED FROM THE BELIEFS AND PRACTICES OF THE YORUBA, EWE, AKAN, AND KINDRED PEOPLES. London: The Epworth Press, 1949.

Schwab, William B. "Kinship and Lineage among the Yoruba." AFRICA, 25 (1955), 352-74.

----------"The Growth and Conflicts of Religion in a ModernYoruba Community." ZAIRE, 6 (1942), 829-35.

DISSERTATIONS AND THESIS ON THE YORUBA

Adedeji, Joel Adeyinka. "The Alarinjo Theatre." Diss., Ibadan, 1969.

Balistreri, June Clara. "The Traditional Elements of the Yoruba Alarinjo Theatre in Wole Soyinka's Plays." Diss., Univ. of Colorado at Boulder, 1978.

180

Corbett, Delbert Franklin. "Theatrical Elements of Traditional Nigerian Drama." Diss., Univ. of Oregon, 1980.

Ezeokoli, Victoria C. "African Theatre: A Nigerian Prototype." Diss., Yale Univ., 1972.

Gibbs, James M. "Aspects of the Nigerian Dramatic Tradition." M.A. Thesis, American Univ., 1967

Graham-White, Anthony. "West African Drama: Folk, Popular, and Literary." Diss., Sandford Univ., 1969.

IyI-Eweka, Ademola. "The Development of Dramatic Troupes in Benin (Nigeria)." Diss., Univ. of Wisconsin-Madison, 1979.

Maccami, Robert. "Traditionalism in the work of Wole Soyinka." M.A. Thesis,Univ. of Ghana, 1969.

Ogunba, Oyinade. "Ritual Drama of the Ijebu People: A Study of Indigenous Festivals." Diss., Ibadan, 1967.

Okpaku, Joseph O. "From Swamp Dwellers to Madmen and Specialists: The Drama of Wole Soyinka." Diss., Standford Univ., 1978.

Olatoregun, J.O. "Traditional Drama in Western Nigeria." Diss., Ibadan, 1965.

Owomoyela,Oyekan. "Folklore and the Rise of Theatre Among the Yoruba." Diss., U.C.L.A., 1970.

Owusu, Martin. "Drama of the Gods: Myth and Ritual in Seven West African Plays." Diss., Brandeis Univ., 1979.

Uyovbukerhi, Atiboroko S.A. "The Idea of Tragic Form in Nigerian Drama Written in English." Diss., Univ. of Wisconsin-Madison, 1976.

GENERAL LISTING - BOOKS

Adedeji, Adebayo. AN INTRODUCTION TO WESTERN NIGERIA: ITS PEOPLE, CULTURE AND SYSTEM OF GOVERNMENT. Ife: University of Ife Press, 1966.

Banham, Martin and Clive Wake. AFRICAN THEATRE TODAY. London: Pittman, 1976.

Chatterji, Suniti Kumar. THE CULTURE AND RELIGION OF THE YORUBAS OF WEST AFRICA. Calcutta: Swami Pavitrananda, 1945.

Cook, David. AFRICAN LITERATURE: A CRITICAL VIEW. London: Longman, 1977.

Crowder, Michael. A SHORT HISTORY OF NIGERIA. New York: Frederick A. Praeger, 1962.

Fadipe, N.A. THE SOCIOLOGY OF THE YORUBA. London: Studio, 1972.

Graham-White, Anthony. THE DRAMA OF BLACK AFRICA. New York: Samuel French, 1974.

Idowu, E. Bolaji. OLADUMARE: GOD IN YORUBA BELIEF. London: Longman, 1962.

Jones, Eldred D., ed. AFRICAN LITERATURE TODAY: NO 8 DRAMA IN AFRICA. New York: Africana Pub. Co., 1976.

182

----------WOLE SOYINKA. New York: Twayne, 1971.

----------THE   WRITINGS   OF   WOLE   SOYINKA.   London:
Heinemann, 1973.

Keribo, O. HISTORY OF THE YORUBA   University Press, 1978.

---------- THE MOVEMENT OF TRANSITION. Ibadan: Ibadan
University press, 1975.

Okpaku, Joseph. CONTEMPORARY AFRICAN   DRAMA: A CRITICAL
ANTHOLOGY. New York: Negro University Press, 1970.

Olaleye, Amos. A PHILOSOPHY OF THE YORUBA RELIGION.
Washington, D.C.: Howard University Press, 1956.

Roscoe, Adrian. MOTHER IS GOLD. New York: Cambridge
University Press, 1971.

Soyinka, Wole. MYTH, LITERATURE AND THE AFRICAN WORLD.
New York: Cambridge University Press, 1976.

----------"The Fourth Stage." THE MORALITY OF ART, ed.
D.W. Jefferson. New York: Barnes and Noble, 1969.

Taiwo, Oladele. AN INTRODUCTION TO WEST AFRICAN
LITERATURE. New Jersey: Nelson, 1967.

GENERAL LISTING - ARTICLES

Abimbola, Wande. "Yoruba Oral Literature: The Place of
Ifa Traditional Religion." AFRICAN NOTES, 2 April, 1965,
pp. 12-16.

Adedeji, Joel A. "The Church and the Emergence of the Nigerian Theatre, 1866-1914." JOURNAL OF THE HISTORICAL SOCIETY OF NIGERIA, IV, No.1 Dec., 1971, pp. 23-45.

----------"Form and the function of Satire in Yoruba Drama." ODU (Ibadan), IV, No, 1, 1967, pp. 61-72.

----------"Oral Tradition and the Contemporary Theatre in Nigeria." RESEARCH IN AFRICAN LITERATURES, II, No 2 Fall, 1971, pp. 134-49.

----------"The Origin and the Form of the Yoruba Masque Theatre." CASHIERS DIETUDES AFRICAINES, XII, No. 2 (46), 1972, pp. 254-76.

----------"The Origin of the Yoruba Masque Theatre: The use of the Ifa Divination Corpus as Historical Evidence." AFRICAN NOTES, VI, No. 1 1970, pp. 70-86.

----------"The Place of Drama in Yoruba Religious Observance." ODU, July 1966, pp. 88-94.

----------"A Profile of Nigerian Theatre: 1960-1970." NIGERIA MAGAZINE, No. 107-9, Dec., 1970-Aug., 1971, pp.3-14.

----------"Traditional Yoruba Theatre." AFRICAN ARTS, III, No. 1, Autumn, 1969, pp. 60-63.

----------"Trends in the content and form of the Opening Glee in Yoruba Drama." RESEARCH IN AFRICAN LITERATURES, IV, No. 1, Spring, 1973,pp. 32-47.

Adeligba, Dapo. "Trance and Theatre: The Nigerian Experience." UFAHAMU, 6, No. 2, 1976, pp. 47-61.

Akaraogun, Alan. "Wole Soyinka." SPEAR MAGAZINE, May 1966, pp. 13-19.

Akinrinsola, F. "Ogun Festival." NIGERIA MAGAZINE, No. 85, June 1965, pp. 85-95.

Alagoa, E.J. "Delta Masquerades." NIGERIA MAGAZINE, No. 93, June 1967, pp. 145-55.

Axworthy, Geoffrey. "The Arts Theatre and the School of Drama." IBADAN, No. 18, Feb. 1964, pp. 62-64.

Banham, Martin. "African Literature II: Nigerian Dramatists in English and the Traditional Nigerian Theatre." JOURNAL OF COMMONWEALTH LITERATURE, III July 1967, pp. 97-102.

----------"Drama in the Commonwealth: Nigeria." NEW THEATRE MAGAZINE, July 1960, pp. 18-21.

----------"Notes on Nigerian Theatre: 1966." BULLETIN OF THE ASSOCIATION FOR AFRICAN LITERATURE IN ENGLISH, IV March 1966, pp. 31-36.

----------"Theatre on Wheels." AFRICAN FORUM, Summer, 1965, pp. 108-9.

Bascom, William R. "The Sociological Role of the Yoruba Cult-Group." AMERICAN ANTHROPOLOGIST, 46, 1944, pp. 64-81.

Beir, H.U. "The Egungun Cult." NIGERIA MAGAZINE, No. 51, 1956, pp. 380-92.

----------"The Egungun Cult Among the Yoruba." PRESENCE AFRICAINE, No. 17-18, Feb.-May 1958, pp. 33-36.

---------"Gelede Mask." ODU, No. 4, 1956, pp. 16-32.

----------"Spirit Children Among the Yoruba." AFRICAN AFFAIRS, 53, No. 213 Oct. 1954, pp. 328-31.

----------"Yoruba Enclava." NIGERIA, No. 58 1958, pp. 238-51.

----------"Yoruba Folk Operas." AFRICAN MUSIC, No.1 1954, pp. 32-34.

Carroll, K.F. "Focus on Race: Yoruba." WORLD MISSION, 16, Summer, 1965, pp. 64-70.

Clark, Ebun. "Ogunde Theatre: The Rise of Contemporary Professional Theatre in Nigeria 1946-72." NIGERIA MAGAZINE, No. 114-16 1974, pp. 3-14, 9-33.

----------"The Nigerian Theatre and the Nationalist Movement: Part III." NIGERIA MAGAZINE, No. 115-16 Dec. 1974, pp. 24-33.

Clark J.P. "Aspects of Nigerian Drama." NIGERIA MAGAZINE, No. 89 June 1966, pp. 118-26.

----------"Our Literary Critics." NIGERIA MAGAZINE, No. 74 Sept. 1962, pp. 79-82.

Clurman, Harold "Theatre." THE NATION, 26, April 1968, pp. 581.

De La Barde, R. "The Ijebu-Ekine Cult." AFRICAN ARTS, 7, Autumn, 1973, pp. 28-33.

186

Echeruo, Michael. "Concert and Theatre in Late Nineteenth Century Lagos." NIGERIA MAGAZINE, No. 74 Sept. 1962, pp. 68-74.

Edmonds, R. and I.C. Edmonds. "Playmakers in Africa." INSTITUTE OF INTERNATIONAL EDUCATION NEWS BULLETIN, 34, May 1959, pp. 20-28.

Ekom, Ernest "The Development of Theatre in Nigeria, 1960-1967." JOURNAL OF NEW AFRICAN LITERATURE AND ARTS, Summer/Fall, 1971, pp. 36-49.

Enfkwe, Ossie Onuora. "Theatre in NIgeria: The Modern Vs. the Traditional." YALE/THEATRE, 8, No. 1, 1976, pp. 62-66.

Ferguson, John. "Nigerian Drama in English." MODERN DRAMA, May 1978, pp. 10-28.

Harper, Peggy. "Dance and Drama in the North." NIGERIA MAGAZINE, No. 94 Sept. 1967, pp. 219-25.

----------"Traditional Dance and New Theatre." AFRICAN NOTES, No. 1 Oct. 1964, pp. 15-16.

Herskovits, Melville J. "Dramatic Expression Among Primitive Peoples." YALE REVIEW, 33, pp. 683-98.

Hill, G. "Reviews." JOURNAL OF COMMONWEALTH LITERATURE, Sept. 1965, pp. 172-74.

Ilogu, C.E. "Changing Religious Beliefs in Nigeria." NIGERIA MAGAZINE, No. 117-18, 1975, pp. 3-20.
Jones, Eldred, D. "The Essential Soyinka." INTRODUCTION TO NIGERIAN LITERATURE, 1971, pp. 43-52.

----------"Progress and Civilization in the Work of Wole Soyinka." PERSPECTIVE ON AFRICAN LITERATURE, 1971, pp. 29-37.

Jones, D.A. "Soyinka." NEW STATESMAN, 72, July 1966, pp. 63-64.

Kolade, Christopher. "Looking at Drama in Nigeria." AFRICAN FORUM, I, Winter, 1966, pp. 77-79.

Larson, Charles R. "Nigerian Drama Comes of Age." AFRICA REPORT, 13, May 1968, pp. 77-78.

Lawal, Babatunde. "Ogun." NIGERIA MAGAZINE, No. 92 March 1967, p. 75.

Lindfors, Bernth. "Nigerian Drama in American Libraries." AFRO-ASIAN THEATRE BULLETIN, 3, Feb. 1968, pp. 22-27.

----------"A Preliminary Checklist of Nigerian Drama In English." AFRO-ASIAN THEATRE BULLETIN, 2, Feb. 1967, pp. 16-21.

Lloyd, P.C. "Yrouba Myths--a Sociologist's Interpretation." ODU, 2, 1955, pp. 20-28.

----------"The Yoruba of Nigeria." PEOPLES OF AFRICA, 1975, pp. 549-82.

McDowell, Robert E. "African Drama, West and South." AFRICA TODAY, 15, Aug./Sept. 1968, pp. 25-28.

Maclean, Una. "Soyinka's International Drama." BLACK ORPHEUS, 15, 1964, pp. 46-51.

Macrow, Donald. "Folk Opera." NIGERIA MAGAZINE, No. 44, 1954, pp. 329-45.

Mahood, M.M. and Phebean Ogundipe. "Wole Soyinka." BLACK ORPHEUS, 15, Aug. 1964, pp. 46-52.

Oduneye, Bayo. "Theatre in Ibadan." CULTURAL EVENTS IN AFRICA, 21, Aug. 1966, pp. i-ii.

Ogunba, Oyin. "Language in an Age of Transition:*lm25 Shakespeare and Soyinka." JOURNAL OF THE NIGERIA ENGLISH STUDIES ASSOCIATION, 6, May 1974, pp. 107-18.

----------"The Agemo Cult in Ijebuland." NIGERIA MAGAZINE, No. 86, 1965, pp. 176-86.

----------"Traditional Content of the Plays of Wole Soyinka." AFRICAN LITERATURE TODAY, 4, 1970, pp. 2-18.

----------"Theatre in Nigeria." PRESENCE AFRICAINE, 58, 1966, pp. 61-88.

Ogunba, Oyinade. "The Poetic Content and Form of Yoruba Occasional Festival Songs." AFRICAN NOTES, 2, 1971, pp. 10-30.

Olafeoye, Tayo. "Cultural Conventions in Soyinka's Art." BA SHIRU, 7, 1976, pp. 67-70.

Omotoso, Kole. "Politics, Propaganda, and Prostitution of Literature." IOWA REVIEW, 7, 1976, pp. 238-45.

O'Neal, John. "Theatre in Yorubaland: An American's Impression." BLACK WORLD, July 1970, pp. 39-48.

Osofisan, Femi. "Tiger on Stage: Wole Soyinka and Nigerian Theatre." In Oyin Ogunba's THEATRE IN AFRICA, Ibadan: Ibadan Univ. Press, 1978, pp. 151-75.

Owomoyela, Oyekan. "Folklore and Yoruba Theatre." RESEARCH IN AFRICAN LITERATURE, 2, Fall, 1971, pp. 121-33.

----------"Yoruba-language Theatre Draws Inspiration from Tradition." AFRICAN REPORT, 15, June 1970, pp. 32-33.

Pieterse, Cosmo. "Dramatic Riches." THE JOURNAL OF COMMONWEALTH LITERATURE, 2, Dec. 1966, pp. 168-71.

Povey, John F. "West African Drama in English." COMPARATIVE DRAMA, 1, Summer, 1967, pp. 110-21.

----------"Wole Soyinka and the Nigerian Drama." TRI-QUARTERLY, 5, Spring 1966, pp. 129-35.

----------"Wole Soyinka: Two Nigerian Comedies." COMPARATIVE DRAMA, 3, Summer 1969, pp. 120-32.

Reckord, B. "Notes on Two Nigerian Playwrights." NEW AFRICA, 4, Sept. 1965, p. 175.

Shideler, Jack. "African Theatre Budding." THE CHRISTIAN SCIENCE MONITOR, march 1967, p. 5.

Soyinka, Wole. "Amos Tutuola on Stage." IBADAN, 16, June 1963, pp. 23-24.

----------"Towards a True Theatre." NIGERIA MAGAZINE, No. 75, Dec. 1962, pp. 58-60.

----------"Theatre in Nigeria." CULTURAL EVENTS IN AFRICA, 5, p. i.

Verger, Pierre. "The Yoruba High God: A Review of the Sources." ODU, 2. Jan. 1966. pp. 19-40.

INDEX